Grade 8

Credits

Illustrations: Laurie Conley, Eric Hammond, Marty Husted, Matt LeBarre, Zeke Smith, Jane Yamada; Page 144: www.shutterstock.com, illagora

Photos: Page 19: www.photos.com; Page 20: Ableimages/Lifesize/Thinkstock; Page 21: www.istockphoto.com/aabejon; Pages 22, 120: Creatas images/Thinkstock; Page 23: www.shutterstock.com, Denise Kappa; Page 24: Creatas/Thinkstock; Pages 25, 27, 126: iStockphoto/Thinkstock; Page 26: Jupiterimages/Brand X Pictures/Thinkstock; Page 28: www.istockphoto.com/bonniej; Page 86: www.shutterstock.com, PHOTOCREO Michael Bednarek; Page 118: Blend Images/Thinkstock; Page 122: Digital Vision/Thinkstock; Page 124: Toby Burrows/Digital Vision/Thinkstock; Page 155: NASA

ISBN 978-0-8454-7576-8

Copyright © 2013 The Continental Press, Inc.

No part of this publication may be reproduced in any form or by any means, electronic, mechanical, photocopying, recording, or otherwise, without the prior written permission of the publisher. All rights reserved. Printed in the United States of America.

Table of Contents

About *Continental's* New York ELLs 4

UNIT 1 Speaking 5

Lesson 1 Social and Academic Interaction 6
Lesson 2 Sentence Completion 9
Lesson 3 Picture Description 19
Lesson 4 Response to Graphic Information 29
Lesson 5 Storytelling 39

UNIT 2 Listening 49

Lesson 6 Word/Sentence Comprehension 50
Lesson 7 Comprehension of Dialogue and Information 2 55
Lesson 8 Listening for Academic Content 65

UNIT 3 Reading 75

Lesson 9   Short Reading Comprehension 76
Lesson 10 Comprehension 86

UNIT 4 Writing 109

Lesson 11 Mechanics and Structure 1 110
Lesson 12 Mechanics and Structure 2 114
Lesson 13 Descriptive Writing Paragraph 118
Lesson 14 Fact-Based Essay 128

UNIT 5 Transition to ELA 153

Session 1 Informational 154
Session 2 Literary 165

About *Continental's* New York ELLs

Continental's New York ELLs workbook works with the NY Learning Standards for English as a Second Language and helps you become familiar with the types of questions you will see on state tests: multiple choice, short written response, extended written response, and oral response.

The book is divided into five units. The first four units practice the skills needed to answer speaking, listening, reading, and writing questions. Unit 5 of the book shows you the passage types and comprehension skills you will need to know as you work with the state ELA standards. There are examples of informational, literary, and functional passages in the book.

Unit	Expectations	Question Type	Scoring
1 Speaking	You will speak answers to questions asked about pictures.	• Oral response • Given one on one	• Scored by administrator • Rubrics provided in back of teacher's edition
2 Listening	You will listen to information read by the administrator or on an audio CD and answer questions about it.	• Multiple choice • Given as a group	• Fill in responses in book or use answer sheets • Scoring sheets provided in back of teacher's edition
3 Reading	You will read short and long passages and answer questions about them.	• Multiple choice • Given as a group	• Fill in responses in book or use answer sheets • Scoring sheets provided in back of teacher's edition
4 Writing	You will answer questions about mechanics and write answers to explain pictures and graphics.	• Multiple choice • Written response • Given as a group	• Fill in responses in book or use answer sheets • Write answers to questions in book • Rubrics provided in back of teacher's edition
5 Transition to ELA	You will read informational and literary passages and answer questions about them.	• Multiple choice • Written response • Given as a group	• Fill in responses in book or use answer sheets • Write answers to questions in book • Rubrics provided in back of teacher's edition

SPEAKING

LESSON 1
Standards 1, 2, 4

Social and Academic Interaction
- listen to a question asked by your teacher
- answer the question out loud

LESSON 2
Standards 1, 2, 4, 5

Sentence Completion
- listen to the beginning of a sentence about a picture
- finish the sentence out loud by describing what is happening in the picture

LESSON 3
Standards 1, 2, 3, 4, 5

Picture Description
- listen to a two-part question about a picture
- use the picture to help you answer the question
- say the answers to both parts of the question out loud

LESSON 4
Standards 1, 3

Response to Graphic Information
- listen to two questions about a chart, table, map, or graph
- use the graphic to help you answer the questions
- say the answers to the questions out loud

LESSON 5
Standard 2

Storytelling
- look at three pictures and understand what they show
- tell a story out loud about the pictures
- tell what happened using the words **first**, **next**, and **last**

Social and Academic Interaction

Directions
Imagine that you and I are having a conversation. I will say something to you. Listen and then answer.

1. What is the name of your school?

2. How many brothers and sisters do you have?

3. Who is your favorite character in a book, and why?

4. What do you do at a library?

5. What do you do after school?

6. Tell me about your favorite room in your house.

7. What do you do when you are tired?

8. What can people do at a mall?

9. What animal makes the best pet, and why?

10. Tell me about a sport you like to play.

Social and Academic Interaction

Directions
Imagine that you and I are having a conversation. I will say something to you. Listen and then answer.

11. When does the school day begin?

12. What activities do you like to do on a rainy day?

13. What does a bicycle look like?

14. Why do people plant gardens?

15. What might someone keep in a bedroom closet?

16. What is your favorite television program, and why?

17. What foods do you like to buy at the supermarket?

18. Why do people have pets?

19. Tell me about where you would like to go on vacation.

20. What might you do in a park?

Social and Academic Interaction

Directions
Imagine that you and I are having a conversation. I will say something to you. Listen and then answer.

21. What might people do to cool off on a hot summer day?

22. Where do people go to eat?

23. Tell me about something that makes you laugh.

24. What does a dentist do?

25. What are some ways students can get to school?

26. Why do people have kitchens?

27. How do you celebrate your favorite holiday?

28. Tell me about what you like to do on the weekend.

29. Which season is the coldest?

30. Why might someone go to a hospital?

Sentence Completion

LESSON 2 *Speaking*

Directions
Look at the words above the picture. Read them silently as they are read out loud. Then look at the picture and finish the sentence. Use the picture to help you choose your words.

1. The boy is teaching his brother to play chess, so…

UNIT 1 Speaking

Sentence Completion

Directions
Look at the words above the picture. Read them silently as they are read out loud. Then look at the picture and finish the sentence. Use the picture to help you choose your words.

2. On a sunny day, the family climbed on their bikes and…

UNIT 1 Speaking

Sentence Completion

Directions
Look at the words above the picture. Read them silently as they are read out loud. Then look at the picture and finish the sentence. Use the picture to help you choose your words.

3. The swimming pool was crowded, so the lifeguard…

UNIT 1 Speaking

Sentence Completion

Directions
Look at the words above the picture. Read them silently as they are read out loud. Then look at the picture and finish the sentence. Use the picture to help you choose your words.

4. School is over, and the friends…

UNIT 1 Speaking

Sentence Completion

Directions
Look at the words above the picture. Read them silently as they are read out loud. Then look at the picture and finish the sentence. Use the picture to help you choose your words.

5. Four students are working on their social studies project, and they…

UNIT 1 Speaking

Sentence Completion

Directions
Look at the words above the picture. Read them silently as they are read out loud. Then look at the picture and finish the sentence. Use the picture to help you choose your words.

6. It was Earth Day, and the volunteers...

14   **UNIT 1**   Speaking ★   © The Continental Press, Inc.   **DUPLICATING THIS MATERIAL IS ILLEGAL.**

Sentence Completion

Directions
Look at the words above the picture. Read them silently as they are read out loud. Then look at the picture and finish the sentence. Use the picture to help you choose your words.

7. The weather is finally warm, so the family…

UNIT 1 Speaking

2 Speaking

Sentence Completion

Directions
Look at the words above the picture. Read them silently as they are read out loud. Then look at the picture and finish the sentence. Use the picture to help you choose your words.

8. On Mother's Day, the little girl…

UNIT 1 Speaking

Sentence Completion

2 Speaking

Directions
Look at the words above the picture. Read them silently as they are read out loud. Then look at the picture and finish the sentence. Use the picture to help you choose your words.

9. As the boy got on the bus, he thought…

UNIT 1 Speaking

2 Speaking

Sentence Completion

Directions
Look at the words above the picture. Read them silently as they are read out loud. Then look at the picture and finish the sentence. Use the picture to help you choose your words.

10. The car won't start, and the young man…

18   UNIT 1   Speaking

Picture Description

LESSON 3 *Speaking*

Directions
Look at the picture. Listen to the question about the picture. Then answer the question. Be sure to answer both parts of the question.

1. What is the man doing, and what might the girl say to him?

© The Continental Press, Inc. DUPLICATING THIS MATERIAL IS ILLEGAL.   ★ UNIT 1 Speaking 19

3 Speaking

Picture Description

Directions
Look at the picture. Listen to the question about the picture. Then answer the question. Be sure to answer both parts of the question.

2. What are the students doing, and why?

Picture Description

Directions
Look at the picture. Listen to the question about the picture. Then answer the question. Be sure to answer both parts of the question.

3. What are the boys doing, and what are they saying to each other?

3 Speaking

Picture Description

Directions
Look at the picture. Listen to the question about the picture. Then answer the question. Be sure to answer both parts of the question.

4. What are the girls doing, and what might the one girl say to the other girl?

22 UNIT 1 Speaking

Picture Description

Directions
Look at the picture. Listen to the question about the picture. Then answer the question. Be sure to answer both parts of the question.

5. Who are these people, and what is the little girl saying?

© The Continental Press, Inc.   DUPLICATING THIS MATERIAL IS ILLEGAL.   ★   UNIT 1   Speaking   **23**

3 Speaking

Picture Description

Directions
Look at the picture. Listen to the question about the picture. Then answer the question. Be sure to answer both parts of the question.

6. What is the man doing, and what might he be thinking?

Picture Description

Directions
Look at the picture. Listen to the question about the picture. Then answer the question. Be sure to answer both parts of the question.

7. What are they doing, and what is the woman saying to the boy?

Picture Description

Directions
Look at the picture. Listen to the question about the picture. Then answer the question. Be sure to answer both parts of the question.

8. Where are they, and what might the boy be saying to the girl?

26 UNIT 1 Speaking © The Continental Press, Inc. DUPLICATING THIS MATERIAL IS ILLEGAL.

Picture Description

Directions
Look at the picture. Listen to the question about the picture. Then answer the question. Be sure to answer both parts of the question.

9. What are they doing, and what might the girl say to the woman?

UNIT 1 Speaking 27

3 Speaking

Picture Description

Directions
Look at the picture. Listen to the question about the picture. Then answer the question. Be sure to answer both parts of the question.

10. What are they doing, and what might the teacher say to the girl?

28   UNIT 1   Speaking   ★   © The Continental Press, Inc.   DUPLICATING THIS MATERIAL IS ILLEGAL.

Response to Graphic Information

LESSON 4 — *Speaking*

Directions
Look carefully at the map. Listen to the questions about the map. Then answer the questions using the information shown.

1. What does the map show?

   Based on the map, describe the routes you would take to get from Smithtown to New Geneva.

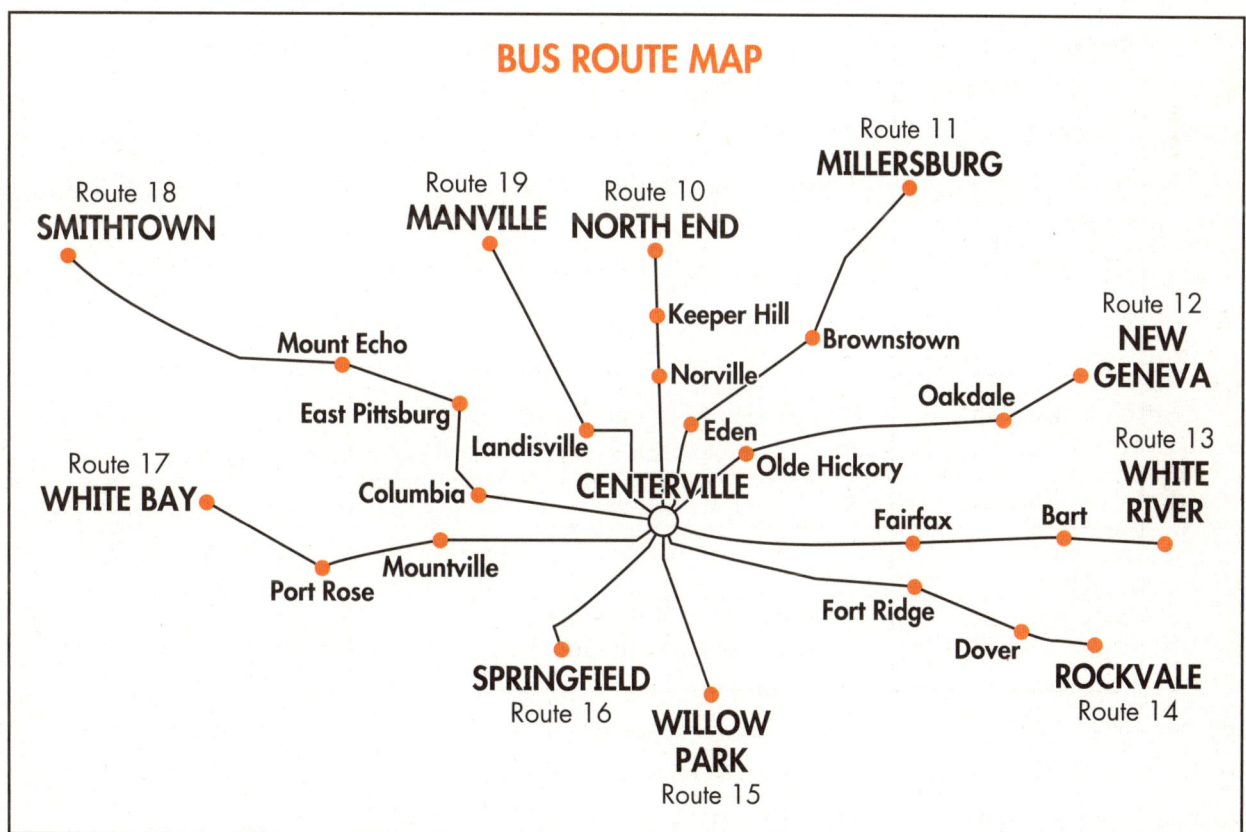

Speaking 4

Response to Graphic Information

Directions
Look carefully at the table. Listen to the questions about the table. Then answer the questions using the information shown.

2. What does the table show?

   Based on the table, how much longer does it take to cook $\frac{1}{2}$ pound of carrots in the microwave than $\frac{1}{2}$ pound of green beans?

MICROWAVE COOKING CHART FOR VEGETABLES

Vegetable	Amount	Cooking Time
Broccoli	$\frac{1}{2}$ pound 1 pound	5 minutes 7 minutes
Green Beans	$\frac{1}{4}$ pound $\frac{1}{2}$ pound	3 minutes 30 seconds 4 minutes 30 seconds
Carrots, sliced	$\frac{1}{4}$ pound $\frac{1}{2}$ pound	4 minutes 30 seconds 6 minutes 30 seconds
Corn	1 ear 2 ears 4 ears	2 minutes 5 minutes 9 minutes

30   UNIT 1   Speaking

Response to Graphic Information

Directions
Look carefully at the graph. Listen to the questions about the graph. Then answer the questions using the information shown.

3. What does the graph show?

    Based on the graph, explain how many gallons of water are wasted in one day.

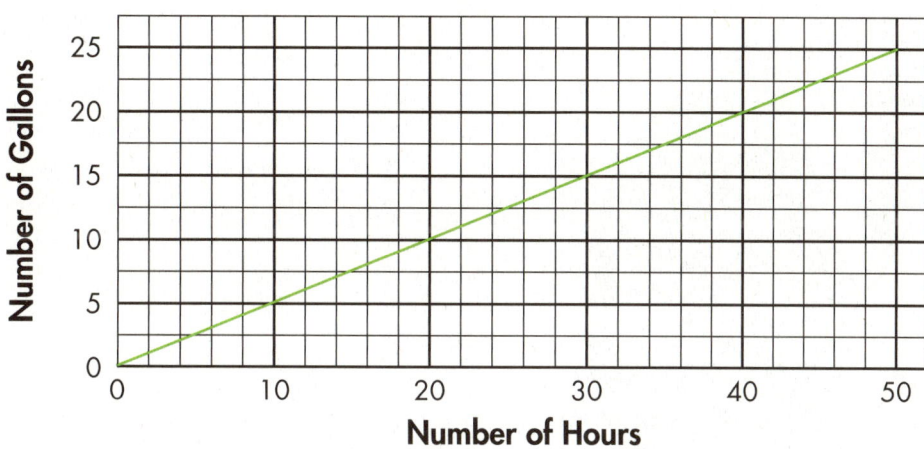

UNIT 1 Speaking 31

Response to Graphic Information

Directions
Look carefully at the chart. Listen to the questions about the chart. Then answer the questions using the information shown.

4. What does the chart show?

   Based on the chart, which types of energy are used more than 20% of the time?

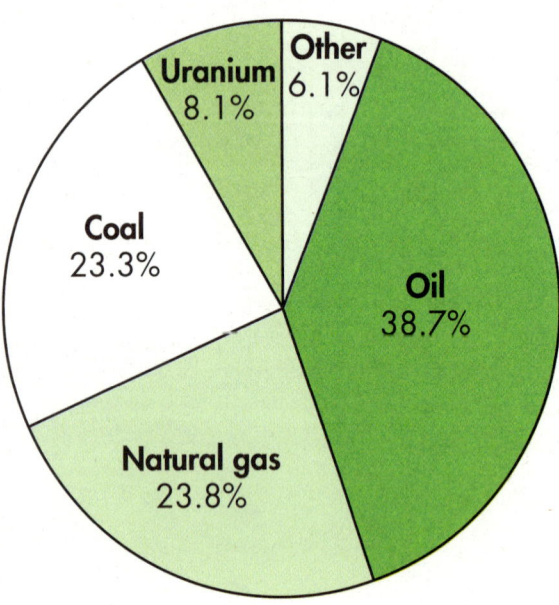

ENERGY USAGE BY SOURCE

Response to Graphic Information

Directions
Look carefully at the map. Listen to the questions about the map. Then answer the questions using the information shown.

5. What does the map show?

   Based on the map, describe the locations of the restrooms in the park so that someone could find one.

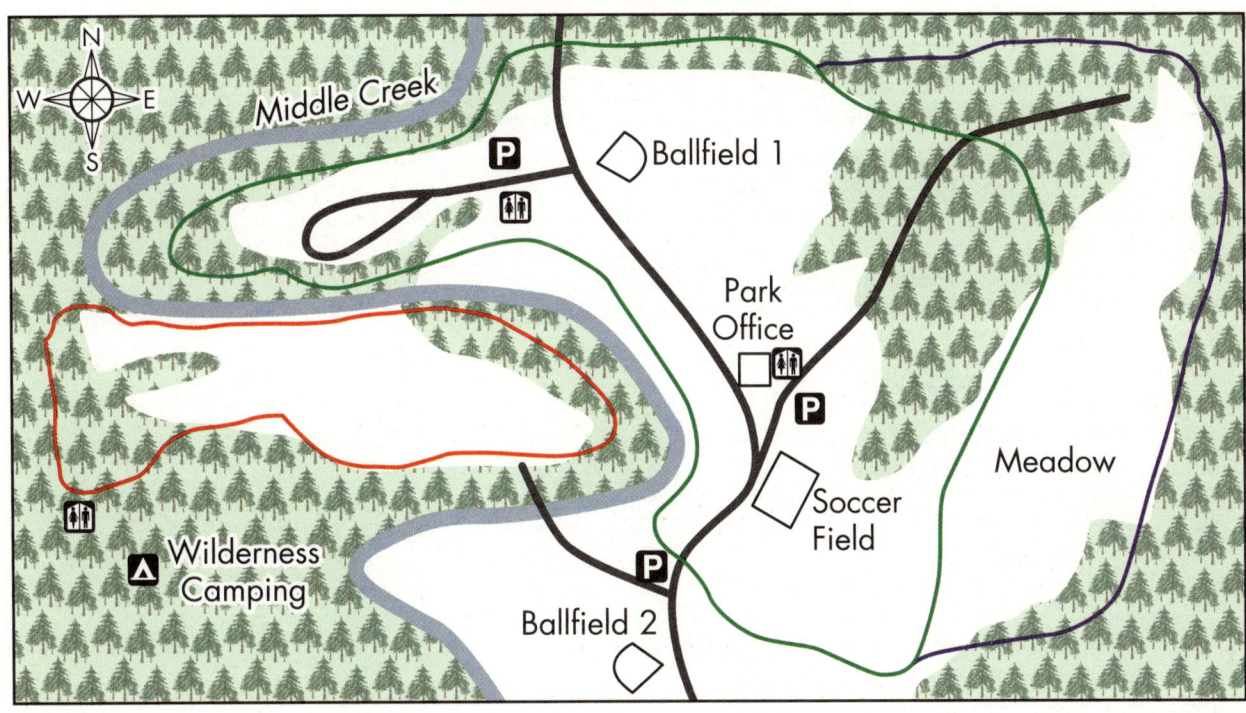

Response to Graphic Information

Directions
Look carefully at the chart. Listen to the questions about the chart. Then answer the questions using the information shown.

6. What does the chart show?

   Based on the chart, compare the lengths of the longest whale and the shortest whale.

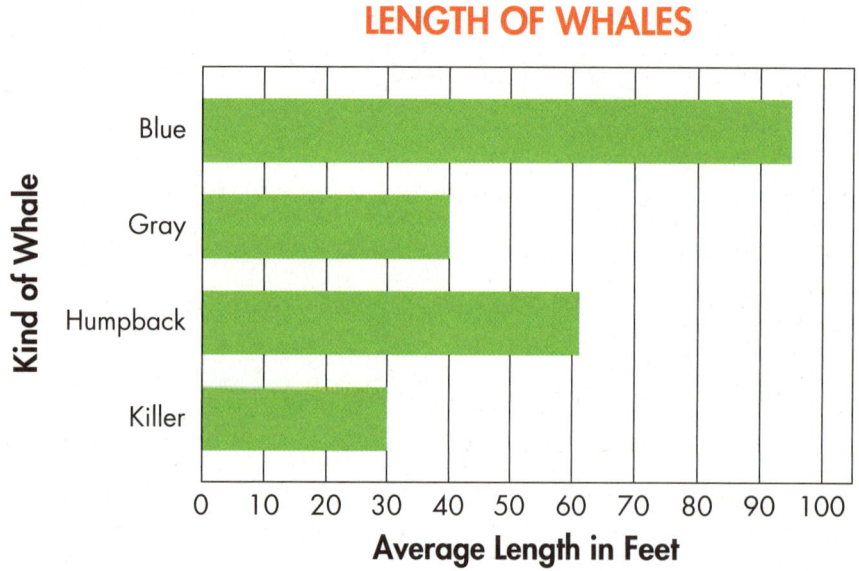

Response to Graphic Information

Directions
Look carefully at the table. Listen to the questions about the table. Then answer the questions using the information shown.

7. What does the table show?

   Based on the table, how does Yolanda's Yogurt compare to Health Farm Yogurt?

NUTRITION OF YOGURT (8-Ounce Serving)

Brand	Fat (Grams)	Sugar (Grams)	Protein (Grams)
Health Farm Yogurt	0	10	9
Contented Cow Yogurt	1	32	9
YoLika Yogurt	2	35	8
Yolanda's Yogurt	3	42	9

Response to Graphic Information

Directions
Look carefully at the graph. Listen to the questions about the graph. Then answer the questions using the information shown.

8. What does the graph show?

   Based on the graph, predict the time the sun will rise on April 13 and explain how you know.

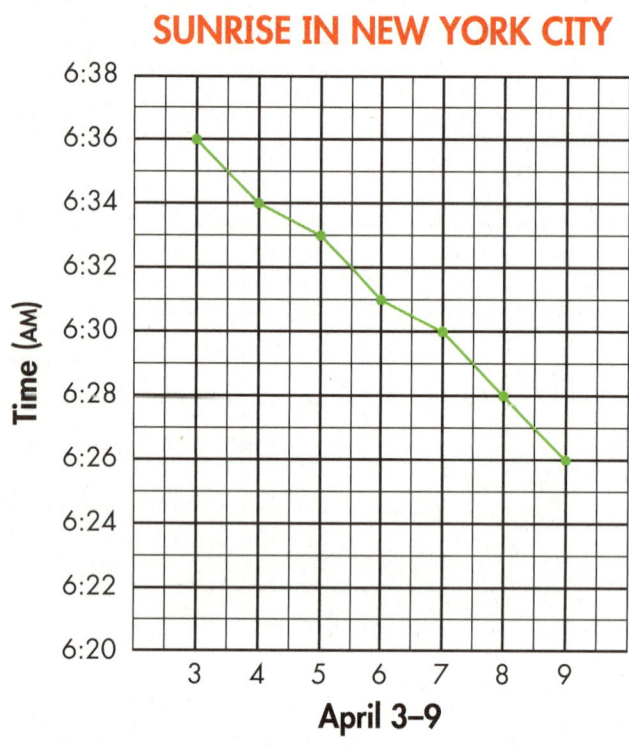

UNIT 1 Speaking

Response to Graphic Information

Directions
Look carefully at the map. Listen to the questions about the map. Then answer the questions using the information shown.

9. What does the map show?

   Based on the map, compare the location of the Hudson River to the location of the Genesee River.

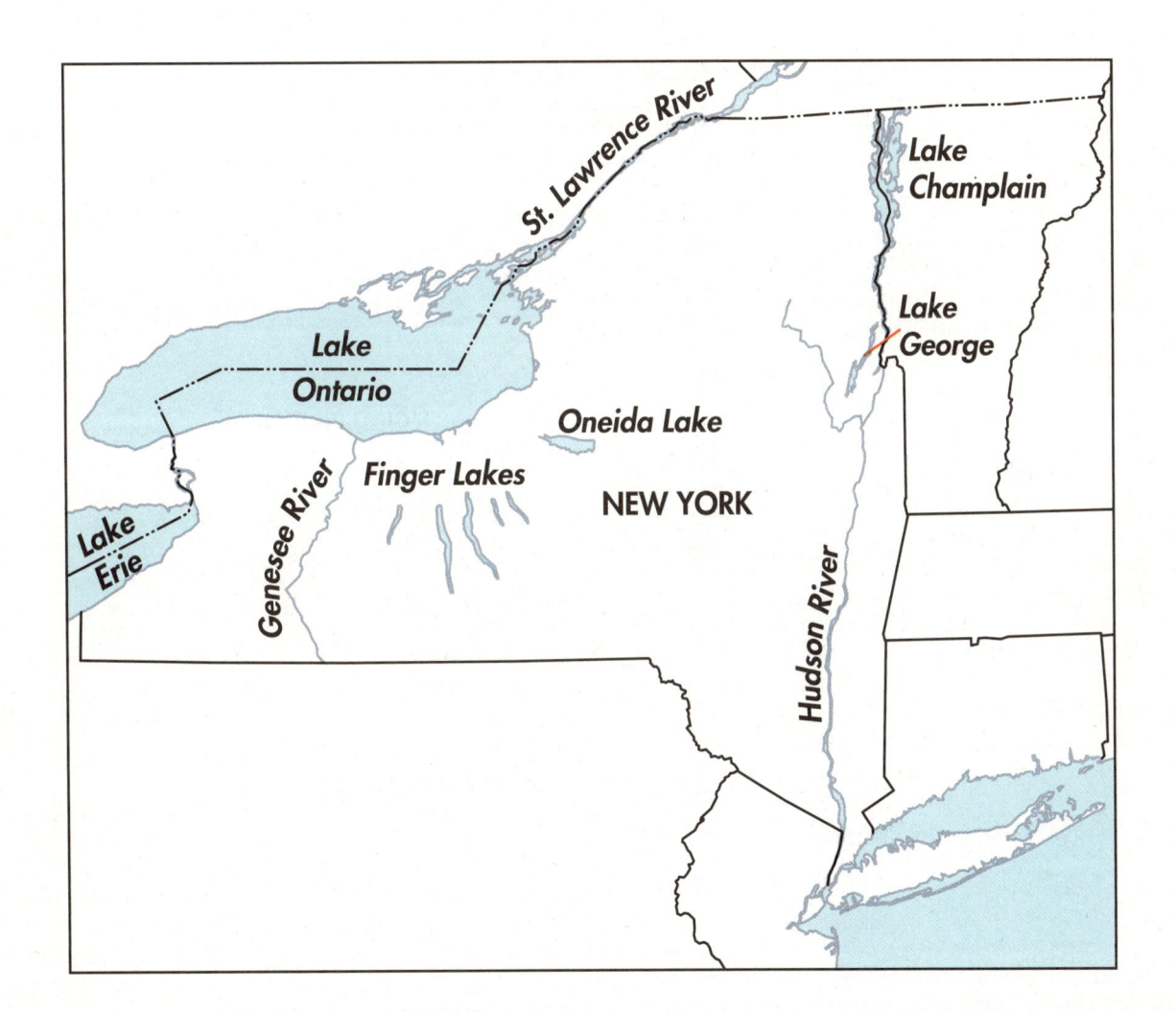

4 Speaking

Response to Graphic Information

Directions
Look carefully at the chart. Listen to the questions about the chart. Then answer the questions using the information shown.

10. What does the chart show?

    Based on the chart, explain how to find the total number of hours Padma spent doing homework.

PADMA'S AFTER-SCHOOL ACTIVITIES FOR ONE MONTH
(120 hours total)

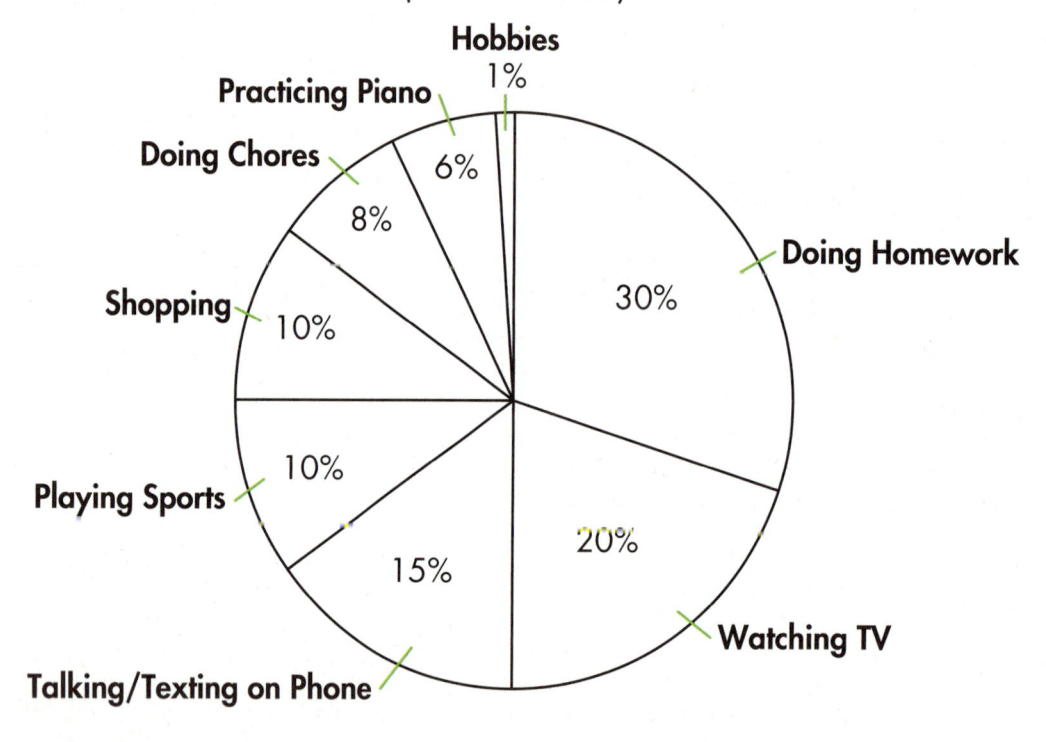

- Hobbies 1%
- Practicing Piano 6%
- Doing Chores 8%
- Shopping 10%
- Playing Sports 10%
- Talking/Texting on Phone 15%
- Watching TV 20%
- Doing Homework 30%

UNIT 1 Speaking

Storytelling

LESSON 5 — *Speaking*

Directions
Look at each picture. Tell a story about what you see in the three pictures. Include as many details as you can. Tell what happened *first*, what happened *next*, and what happened *last*.

1.

First
1

Next
2

Last
3

5 Speaking

Storytelling

Directions
Look at each picture. Tell a story about what you see in the three pictures. Include as many details as you can. Tell what happened *first*, what happened *next*, and what happened *last*.

2.

First
1

Next
2

Last
3

40 UNIT 1 Speaking © The Continental Press, Inc. DUPLICATING THIS MATERIAL IS ILLEGAL.

Storytelling

5 Speaking

Directions
Look at each picture. Tell a story about what you see in the three pictures. Include as many details as you can. Tell what happened *first*, what happened *next*, and what happened *last*.

3.

**First
1**

**Next
2**

**Last
3**

UNIT 1 Speaking 41

5 Speaking

Storytelling

Directions
Look at each picture. Tell a story about what you see in the three pictures. Include as many details as you can. Tell what happened *first*, what happened *next*, and what happened *last*.

4.

First
1

Next
2

Last
3

42 UNIT 1 Speaking

Storytelling

Directions
Look at each picture. Tell a story about what you see in the three pictures. Include as many details as you can. Tell what happened *first*, what happened *next*, and what happened *last*.

5.

First
1

Next
2

Last
3

★ UNIT 1 Speaking 43

5 Speaking

Storytelling

Directions
Look at each picture. Tell a story about what you see in the three pictures. Include as many details as you can. Tell what happened *first*, what happened *next*, and what happened *last*.

6.

**First
1**

**Next
2**

**Last
3**

44   **UNIT 1**   Speaking

Storytelling

Directions
Look at each picture. Tell a story about what you see in the three pictures. Include as many details as you can. Tell what happened *first*, what happened *next*, and what happened *last*.

7.

First
1

Next
2

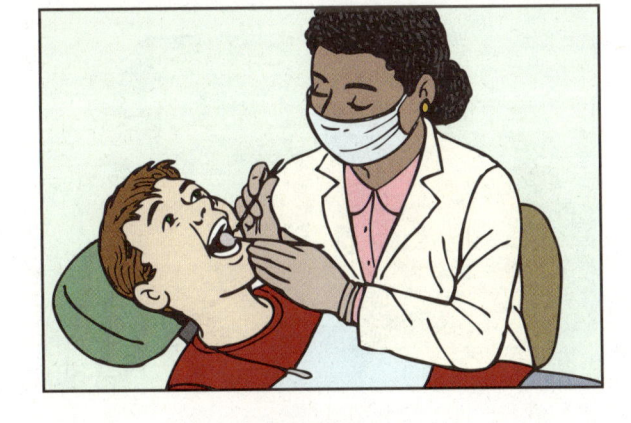

Last
3

UNIT 1 Speaking 45

5 Speaking

Storytelling

Directions
Look at each picture. Tell a story about what you see in the three pictures. Include as many details as you can. Tell what happened *first*, what happened *next*, and what happened *last*.

8.

First
1

Next
2

Last
3

46 UNIT 1 Speaking

Storytelling

Directions
Look at each picture. Tell a story about what you see in the three pictures. Include as many details as you can. Tell what happened *first*, what happened *next*, and what happened *last*.

9.

**First
1**

**Next
2**

**Last
3**

UNIT 1 Speaking

5 Speaking

Storytelling

Directions
Look at each picture. Tell a story about what you see in the three pictures. Include as many details as you can. Tell what happened *first*, what happened *next*, and what happened *last*.

10.

First
1

Next
2

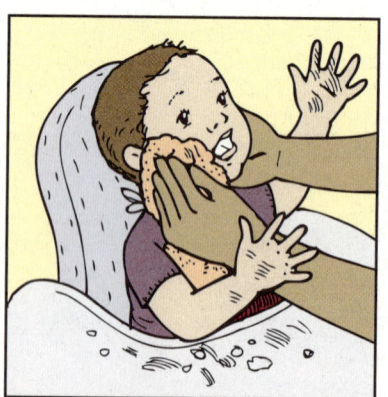

Last
3

48 UNIT 1 Speaking © The Continental Press, Inc. **DUPLICATING THIS MATERIAL IS ILLEGAL.**

Unit 2 LISTENING

LESSON 6
Standard 1

Word/Sentence Comprehension
- look at three pictures
- listen to a question about the pictures
- fill in the correct answer to the question

LESSON 7
Standards 1, 4, 5

Comprehension of Dialogue and Information 2
- listen to a short story and a question about the story
- read the question and answer choices
- fill in the correct answer to the question

LESSON 8
Standard 1

Listening for Academic Content
- listen to a lesson and questions about the lesson
- read the questions and answer choices
- fill in the correct answers to the questions

© The Continental Press, Inc.   DUPLICATING THIS MATERIAL IS ILLEGAL.   ★ UNIT 2   Listening   49

LESSON 6
Listening

Word/Sentence Comprehension

Directions
Listen to the question. Look at the three pictures. Fill in the correct circle.

1.

Ⓐ   Ⓑ   Ⓒ

2.

Ⓐ   Ⓑ   Ⓒ

50 UNIT 2 Listening

Word/Sentence Comprehension

Directions
Listen to the question. Look at the three pictures. Fill in the correct circle.

6 *Listening*

3.

Ⓐ Ⓑ Ⓒ

4.

Ⓐ Ⓑ Ⓒ

★ UNIT 2 Listening 51

Word/Sentence Comprehension

Directions
Listen to the question. Look at the three pictures. Fill in the correct circle.

5.

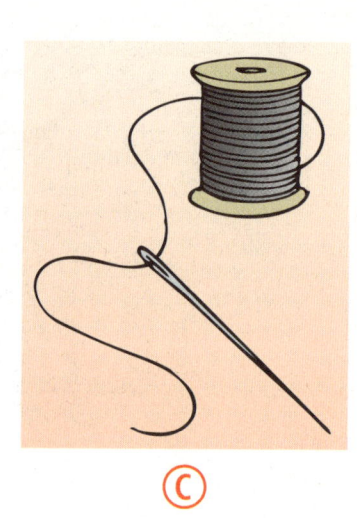

Ⓐ   Ⓑ   Ⓒ

6.

Ⓐ   Ⓑ   Ⓒ

52   UNIT 2   Listening

Word/Sentence Comprehension

6 Listening

Directions
Listen to the question. Look at the three pictures. Fill in the correct circle.

7.

Ⓐ   Ⓑ SQUASH   Ⓒ

8.

Ⓐ   Ⓑ   Ⓒ

UNIT 2   Listening   53

6 Listening

Word/Sentence Comprehension

Directions
Listen to the question. Look at the three pictures. Fill in the correct circle.

9.

Ⓐ   Ⓑ   Ⓒ

10.

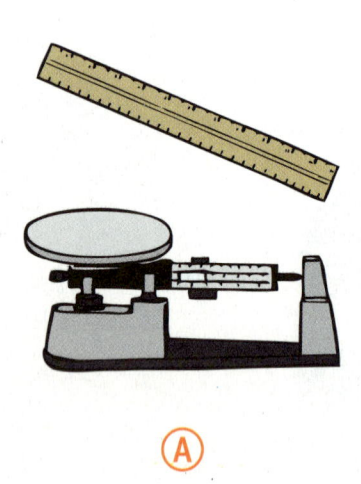

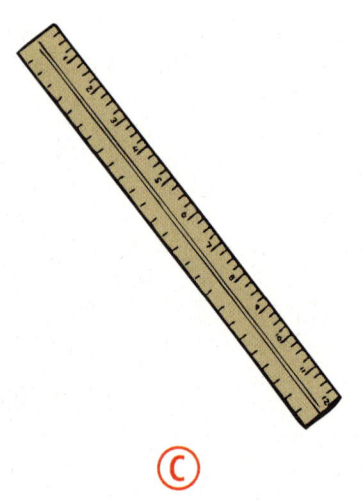

Ⓐ   Ⓑ   Ⓒ

54   **UNIT 2**   Listening   © The Continental Press, Inc.   **DUPLICATING THIS MATERIAL IS ILLEGAL.**

Comprehension of Dialogue and Information 2

LESSON 7 *Listening*

Directions
Listen to the short story. Read the question and answers silently as they are read out loud. Fill in the correct circle.

1. What will Alex do after he helps Mom?
   - Ⓐ Eat lunch
   - Ⓑ Fix his bike
   - Ⓒ Ride to the swimming pool
   - Ⓓ Play video games with his friend

2. Why is Alex fixing his bike?
   - Ⓐ So he can go to school
   - Ⓑ So he can go to the garden
   - Ⓒ So he can visit his friend
   - Ⓓ So he can go swimming

7 Listening

Comprehension of Dialogue and Information 2

Directions
Listen to the short story. Read the question and answers silently as they are read out loud. Fill in the correct circle.

3. Which statement about a cold is true?
   - Ⓐ A person always has symptoms before he or she becomes infected.
   - Ⓑ Cold viruses can't live on computer keyboards.
   - Ⓒ Doorknobs have more cold viruses than any other surface.
   - Ⓓ The most common way it spreads is by person-to-person contact.

4. What is the main idea of this story?
   - Ⓐ Colds are spread by a virus that passes from one person to another.
   - Ⓑ Cold viruses live on things people touch, like doorknobs and computers.
   - Ⓒ Colds are spread mostly by people who don't know they are infected.
   - Ⓓ Cold viruses are mostly spread by coughing and sneezing.

Comprehension of Dialogue and Information 2

Directions
Listen to the short story. Read the question and answers silently as they are read out loud. Fill in the correct circle.

5. Why will the student council start recycling?
    - Ⓐ The local landfill is full.
    - Ⓑ The custodians are complaining.
    - Ⓒ The science club is demanding a recycling program.
    - Ⓓ The council wants to help solve the town's trash problem.

6. What are the middle school students discarding?
    - Ⓐ Glass bottles and metal cans
    - Ⓑ Plastic bottles and paper
    - Ⓒ Paper and glass bottles
    - Ⓓ Metal cans and paper

7 Listening

Comprehension of Dialogue and Information 2

Directions
Listen to the short story. Read the question and answers silently as they are read out loud. Fill in the correct circle.

7. What has Fahd already learned about pets?
   - Ⓐ Dog owners work hardest.
   - Ⓑ Fish are the easiest pets to have.
   - Ⓒ Owners of cats have few responsibilities.
   - Ⓓ Owners of all pets have to accept responsibilities.

8. How is taking care of a cat different from taking care of a dog?
   - Ⓐ Dogs need vaccinations, but cats do not.
   - Ⓑ Only cats have to be fed every day.
   - Ⓒ Only dogs have to be walked every day.
   - Ⓓ Cats need to be played with but dogs do not.

Comprehension of Dialogue and Information 2

7 Listening

Directions
Listen to the short story. Read the question and answers silently as they are read out loud. Fill in the correct circle.

9. What do tomatoes and oranges have in common?
   - (A) Both are vegetables.
   - (B) Both taste sweet.
   - (C) Both are fruits.
   - (D) Both grow on trees.

10. Why do scientists consider the tomato a fruit?
    - (A) It tastes sweet.
    - (B) It grows on a tree.
    - (C) It is never cooked.
    - (D) It develops from a flower.

UNIT 2   Listening

Comprehension of Dialogue and Information 2

Directions
Listen to the short story. Read the question and answers silently as they are read out loud. Fill in the correct circle.

11. Which sentence about seismographs is false?
    - Ⓐ Seismographs help scientists learn more about earthquakes.
    - Ⓑ Seismographs are placed in or near faults.
    - Ⓒ Seismographs measure the magnitude of an earthquake.
    - Ⓓ Seismographs only measure in an up-down direction.

12. What happens second?
    - Ⓐ Scientists study the information.
    - Ⓑ A seismograph is placed near a fault.
    - Ⓒ An earthquake sends out shock waves.
    - Ⓓ The seismograph records the earth movement.

Comprehension of Dialogue and Information 2

Directions
Listen to the short story. Read the question and answers silently as they are read out loud. Fill in the correct circle.

13. What is this story mainly about?
    - Ⓐ Bad weather
    - Ⓑ Thunderstorm safety
    - Ⓒ Thunder and lightning
    - Ⓓ The dangers of thunderstorms

14. What kind of air movement causes thunderstorms to form?
    - Ⓐ Warm air moves downward and cool air moves upward.
    - Ⓑ Warm air moves upward and cool air moves downward.
    - Ⓒ Both warm air and cool air move upward.
    - Ⓓ Both warm air and cool air move downward.

Comprehension of Dialogue and Information 2

Directions
Listen to the short story. Read the question and answers silently as they are read out loud. Fill in the correct circle.

15. How are parallelograms and trapezoids similar?

    Ⓐ Both have four sides, four angles, and at least two parallel sides.

    Ⓑ Both have four sides, four angles, and the opposite sides are parallel.

    Ⓒ Both have four equal sides.

    Ⓓ Both have four equal angles.

16. What is true of a polygon with four equal sides and four equal angles?

    Ⓐ It is a quadrilateral only.

    Ⓑ It is a parallelogram only.

    Ⓒ It is a quadrilateral and a trapezoid.

    Ⓓ It is a quadrilateral and a parallelogram.

Comprehension of Dialogue and Information 2

Directions
Listen to the short story. Read the question and answers silently as they are read out loud. Fill in the correct circle.

17. Why do you think Virgil will enter the essay contest?
    - Ⓐ He wants to win the $500 scholarship.
    - Ⓑ He thinks his ideas are best.
    - Ⓒ He dislikes polluters.
    - Ⓓ He cares about the environment.

18. Which form of transportation is Virgil least likely to use?
    - Ⓐ A car
    - Ⓑ A bus
    - Ⓒ A bike
    - Ⓓ Walking

Comprehension of Dialogue and Information 2

Directions
Listen to the short story. Read the question and answers silently as they are read out loud. Fill in the correct circle.

19. Which animal will probably be chosen as mascot?
    - Ⓐ Lion
    - Ⓑ Eagle
    - Ⓒ Porpoise
    - Ⓓ Horse

20. Why did Laura suggest the eagle?
    - Ⓐ It is intelligent.
    - Ⓑ It is strong.
    - Ⓒ It is playful.
    - Ⓓ It is majestic.

LESSON 8 Listening

Listening for Academic Content

Directions
You will hear a lesson read to you twice. Then you will hear questions about the lesson. Fill in the correct circle for each question.

NOTES

Do not turn the page until you are told to do so.

Listening for Academic Content

1. What is this lesson mainly about?
   - Ⓐ Different kinds of wetlands
   - Ⓑ How wetlands filter water
   - Ⓒ How wetlands prevent floods
   - Ⓓ The importance of wetlands

2. According to the lesson, what is the source of water in a salt wetland?
   - Ⓐ An ocean
   - Ⓑ A river
   - Ⓒ A swamp
   - Ⓓ A lake

Listening for Academic Content

Directions
You will hear a lesson read to you twice. Then you will hear questions about the lesson. Fill in the correct circle for each question.

NOTES

Do not turn the page until you are told to do so.

Listening for Academic Content

3. According to the lesson, what language did the members of the League of Five Nations speak?
   - (A) Mohawk
   - (B) Seneca
   - (C) Iroquois
   - (D) Onondaga

4. What is this lesson mainly about?
   - (A) How the government of the League of Five Nations worked
   - (B) Which tribes made up the League of Five Nations
   - (C) Why the League of Five Nations formed
   - (D) Where the tribes of the Five Nations lived

and## Listening for Academic Content

Directions
You will hear a lesson read to you twice. Then you will hear questions about the lesson. Fill in the correct circle for each question.

NOTES

Do not turn the page until you are told to do so.

Listening for Academic Content

5. What is this lesson mainly about?
   - Ⓐ How to play board games
   - Ⓑ The meaning of probability
   - Ⓒ The faces on number cubes
   - Ⓓ Ways to write probability

6. According to the lesson, what is the probability of rolling a 3 on a number cube?
   - Ⓐ One out of three
   - Ⓑ Three out of five
   - Ⓒ One out of six
   - Ⓓ Three out of six

8 Listening

Listening for Academic Content

Directions
You will hear a lesson read to you twice. Then you will hear questions about the lesson. Fill in the correct circle for each question.

NOTES

Do not turn the page until you are told to do so.

UNIT 2 Listening 71

Listening for Academic Content

7. What is this lesson mainly about?
   - Ⓐ The history and growth of education
   - Ⓑ The value of handmade books in Europe
   - Ⓒ The inventions of Johannes Gutenberg
   - Ⓓ The effect of the invention of movable type on the world

8. According to the lesson, where was printing with movable type first invented?
   - Ⓐ China
   - Ⓑ Russia
   - Ⓒ Germany
   - Ⓓ England

Listening for Academic Content

Directions
You will hear a lesson read to you twice. Then you will hear questions about the lesson. Fill in the correct circle for each question.

NOTES

Do not turn the page until you are told to do so.

Listening for Academic Content

9. What is the main idea of this lesson?

   A) Weather and climate are different.

   B) Deserts have hot, dry climates all year round.

   C) An area's climate is determined by several factors.

   D) Mountain ranges are wet on one side and dry on the other.

10. According to the lesson, what determines the amount of sunlight an area receives?

    A) Latitude and altitude

    B) Latitude and mountain ranges

    C) Altitude and prevailing winds

    D) Altitude and large bodies of water

Unit 3 READING

LESSON 9
Standard 1

Short Reading Comprehension
- read a short passage
- read the questions and answer choices after the passage
- fill in the correct answers to the questions

LESSON 10
Standards 1, 2, 3

Comprehension
- read a longer passage
- read the questions and answer choices after the passage
- fill in the correct answers to the questions

Short Reading Comprehension

LESSON 9

Directions
Read the passage. Then answer the questions that follow. Fill in the correct circle.

Nature's Colors

1   Long before people began to record human history, they were making colored paints. Cave paintings dating back more than 30,000 years show that Stone Age people were creating a variety of colors. But they were not the first artists. Pigments and grinding equipment have been found in Africa. These materials may be more than 300,000 years old. That's ten times older than the cave paintings.

2   Natural colors are used in two forms: dyes and pigments. Many dyes come from plants. Dyes are dissolved in a liquid, usually water. They are commonly used to stain materials such as paper, yarns, and leather. Pigments are finely ground solid particles of color mixed in a medium such as oil. They are used to create paint and ink.

3   Natural dyes come in a dazzling array of hues. One of the most famous is Tyrian purple, made from a yellowish secretion of the Murex snail. The slime, when exposed to sunlight, stains things purple. Tyrian purple came into use around 1200 B.C. It was expensive and difficult to produce, though, and soon the color was closely associated with royalty and power.

4   Pigments are often ground from minerals, and many of them were once extremely valuable. Ultramarine blue came from the semiprecious stone called lapis lazuli. Because ultramarine was so costly, artists used to specify in their contracts how much blue would be used in the painting and what kind of blue it would be.

5   Dyes and pigments were made from nature's colors until the 19th century, when scientists discovered how to create synthetic colors in the laboratory.

Short Reading Comprehension

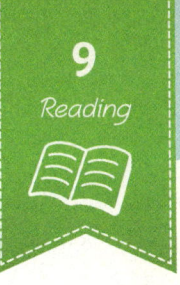

1. Based on information in the passage, what is likely true about most dyes and pigments in use today?

    Ⓐ They are synthetic.

    Ⓑ They come from natural sources.

    Ⓒ They are the same as those used over the centuries.

    Ⓓ They are more beautiful than those used in the past.

2. If you made a time line of the dates from this passage, which of these would be the third entry?

    Ⓐ 19th century

    Ⓑ 300,000 years ago

    Ⓒ 30,000 years ago

    Ⓓ 1200 B.C.

3. What causes the secretion from the Murex snail to turn things purple?

    Ⓐ Slime

    Ⓑ Sunlight

    Ⓒ Mineral pigment

    Ⓓ Water

Short Reading Comprehension

Directions
Read the passage. Then answer the questions that follow. Fill in the correct circle.

The History of the Marathon

1   No doubt, you've heard of marathon races. These long-distance runs cover a little more than 26 miles, and they are held all over the country and the world. Three of the most famous marathons are in Boston, New York, and London. The most famous marathon of all time, however, was in Greece. It took place thousands of years ago, and it is not clear whether it really happened or is a legend.

2   To call that first marathon a race is a bit misleading. It was actually the course supposedly covered by an army messenger. The man's name was Pheidippides (fy•DIP•i•deez). He fought for Athens in one of the many wars against the Persians. Before the battle began, the soldiers of Athens knew they were outnumbered. This is what first set Pheidippides off and running. He ran to Sparta, about 140 miles away, to seek aid. The Spartans, however, were in the middle of a celebration and would not leave their city until the next full moon.

3   Pheidippedes then ran back to Marathon, where he took part in the battle. He fought bravely, and the outnumbered Greeks held off the Persians. After the victory, Pheidippedes was sent back to Athens to deliver the good news. Legend has it that he achieved his goal, announced the victory with his last breath, and died on the spot.

4   The approximate distance he covered in that final run was 24 miles. When the modern Olympics revived the tradition in Greece in 1896, a form of the marathon race was held. During the 1908 Olympic games in London, the official marathon distance was increased to 26 miles. This was done so that the finish line would be right in front of the royal box where the king's family would see it. Sixteen years later, the distance was changed to 26.2 miles in Paris. This has long been the standard for a full marathon ever since.

Short Reading Comprehension

4. Who were the soldiers of Athens fighting?

    A. The Greeks
    B. The Persians
    C. The Spartans
    D. The British

5. Based on information from the passage, which statement expresses an opinion?

    A. A marathon is an official Olympic event.
    B. No foot race is more grueling than a marathon.
    C. A marathon is a long-distance foot race of 26.2 miles.
    D. Boston, New York, and London hold well-known marathons.

6. The author probably wrote this passage for what purpose?

    A. Persuade the reader to train for a marathon
    B. Entertain the reader with a story from history
    C. Convince the reader to watch the Olympic games
    D. Inform the reader about an interesting topic

Short Reading Comprehension

Directions
Read the passage. Then answer the questions that follow. Fill in the correct circle.

A Celebration of Mexican Pride

1   *Cinco de Mayo* (SINK•oh duh MY•oh) is the name of a holiday in Mexico. The Spanish words mean "fifth of May." The date refers to May 5, 1862. On that day, Mexico defeated France at the Battle of Puebla, a city about 100 miles east of Mexico City. The Mexican army was small. The French army was larger and better equipped. The victory became a source of great pride for Mexicans.

2   People often think that Cinco de Mayo is Mexican Independence Day. It is not. Mexico declared independence from Spain in September 1810. It celebrates Independence Day on September 16. Cinco de Mayo, in fact, is not an official national holiday in Mexico. It is celebrated mostly in the Puebla region.

3   The United States, however, has adopted Cinco de Mayo. The day has become a yearly celebration of Mexican pride and culture. Large Cinco de Mayo festivals are held in cities such as Los Angeles, San Antonio, Denver, and Phoenix. These places are homes to great numbers of people with Mexican ancestry.

4   Each year, Cinco de Mayo celebrations in the United States get bigger and bigger. This is partly because the number of people of Mexican heritage keeps growing. But people of all backgrounds attend and enjoy these events. One of the largest festivals is held in New York. In some years, more than 250,000 people attend it. This huge outdoor festival has live mariachi music and folk dancing. There, people of all backgrounds enjoy Mexican food and games.

Short Reading Comprehension

7. Why are large Cinco de Mayo festivals held in cities like Los Angeles and San Antonio?

    Ⓐ These cities have Spanish names.

    Ⓑ These cities are near Mexico.

    Ⓒ These cities have many people of Mexican heritage.

    Ⓓ These cities have parks that are large enough for festivals.

8. How do Cinco de Mayo and Mexican Independence Day compare?

    Ⓐ They are the same holiday in Mexico.

    Ⓑ Cinco de Mayo is not celebrated anywhere in Mexico.

    Ⓒ Only Cinco de Mayo is celebrated in the United States.

    Ⓓ Only Mexican Independence Day is celebrated in Mexico.

9. Based on this passage, what will probably happen to the Cinco de Mayo holiday?

    Ⓐ It will disappear in Mexico.

    Ⓑ It will continue to spread in the United States.

    Ⓒ It will become an official national holiday in Mexico.

    Ⓓ It will become an official national holiday in the United States.

Short Reading Comprehension

Directions
Read the passage. Then answer the questions that follow. Fill in the correct circle.

The History of Tea

1   Tea is a popular drink. Of course, tea can be made from any kind of herb, flower, or spice that has been steeped in hot water. Genuine tea, however, is made from the leaves of the tea plant, *Camellia sinensis*. This is the tea discovered about 5,000 years ago in China.

2   Although no one knows who first placed dried tea leaves in boiling water, the pleasures of tea drinking quickly spread throughout China. The first book about tea was written about 1,200 years ago by a man named Lu Yu. The Chinese believed tea could give a person energy, bring joy to the spirit, and even improve eyesight. The habit of tea drinking soon spread from China to Japan.

3   In 1556, Father Jasper de Cruz, a priest from Portugal, sailed on a ship to China. He tasted tea while he was there and wrote about it in 1560 when he got home. Portuguese traders brought tea to Europe. Soon Dutch and English ships were carrying the delicious and valuable leaf, too.

4   At first, tea cost an enormous amount of money and for many years, only the rich could afford to buy it. By 1675, though, tea could be bought cheaply in shops throughout Europe. In countries like France and Spain, people came to prefer new drinks made from plants in America and Africa: chocolate and coffee. Settlers in America, however, shared the Dutch and English taste for tea.

5   There are many kinds of tea, and they all have different names: black tea, green tea, orange pekoe, and oolong. All of them, though, are made from the *Camellia sinensis* plant. Terms such as *green tea* and *black tea* describe how the leaves were prepared after harvesting. In green tea, for instance, the leaves have been dried without fermentation, a chemical process. In contrast, black tea is made from leaves that have been fermented.

Short Reading Comprehension

10. In paragraph 1, what does the word <u>steeped</u> mean?

Ⓐ Extremely high

Ⓑ Placed at a rapid incline

Ⓒ Subjected to thoroughly

Ⓓ Soaked in hot water

11. How are green tea and black tea alike?

Ⓐ They are both fermented.

Ⓑ Neither is real tea.

Ⓒ Neither is fermented.

Ⓓ They are both from the same plant.

12. Why did so many Europeans want to buy tea?

Ⓐ Tea was expensive at first.

Ⓑ They thought it was delicious.

Ⓒ Father Jasper de la Cruz wrote about it.

Ⓓ The Chinese and Japanese people liked tea.

Short Reading Comprehension

Directions
Read the passage. Then answer the questions that follow. Fill in the correct circle.

Why Save the Rain Forest?

1   Every year, an area the size of Greece is stripped bare of trees. Most of this woodland is in tropical countries. Much of it is being cleared for farming, even though the soil is poor in nutrients. Farmers in these regions usually can't afford fertilizer, and after two or three years, the soil is worn out. When crops fail, the bare land is abandoned, to be eroded by water. To survive, farmers must then clear more forest.

2   Tropical rain forests grow where the climate is hot and wet. In 1950, they covered 14 percent of our planet's land surface. Most of that land was in Central and South America and the rest in Africa and Southeast Asia. By 1991, over half of this forest had been cleared for farming, livestock grazing, and wood products. A cry went up around the world to "Save the rain forests!" But most rain forests are in poor countries. Farming this land and selling its resources could improve people's lives. Why, then, is the rain forest worth saving?

3   At least 40 percent of the world's plant and animal species live in tropical rain forests. Most of them have not yet been identified by science. The known species include over 2,000 kinds of edible fruit trees. One hectare (2.5 acres) of rain forest may contain over 750 species of trees. That's more than grow in the entire United States. One-fourth of all prescription medicines are made from chemicals extracted from rain forest plants. Less than one percent of rain forest plants have been tested scientifically. Finally, rain forests have been called the lungs of our planet because their trees provide more than 30 percent of the world's oxygen.

4   Environmental experts say that people could make more money by harvesting the useful products of the rain forest than by cutting them down. Nevertheless, nearly 200,000 acres of rain forest continue to be cut or burned every day.

Short Reading Comprehension

13. What is this passage mainly about?
    - Ⓐ Reasons for saving the rain forest
    - Ⓑ Reasons for preserving nature
    - Ⓒ Plants and animals of the rain forest
    - Ⓓ Farming in tropical countries

14. Which of the following steps happens second?
    - Ⓐ Crops fail.
    - Ⓑ The land is eroded by water.
    - Ⓒ The soil becomes worn out.
    - Ⓓ Rain forests are cleared for farming.

15. Based on the article, what probably would not happen as a result of clearing rain forests?
    - Ⓐ There would be less oxygen in the air.
    - Ⓑ Many plants and animal would become extinct.
    - Ⓒ We would lose many possible food plants.
    - Ⓓ Farmers would make more money.

Comprehension

Directions
Read the passage. Then answer the questions that follow. Fill in the correct circle.

The Common Cold

1   Aaaah-CHOOO!

2   You grab a tissue and get it up to your nose just in time. You realize that your nose is starting to run and your throat feels rather scratchy; you suspect you are coming down with a cold.

3   A common cold starts when a virus grows inside your nose. Particles of a virus are very tiny—much smaller than the cells they invade. As these particles multiply in the cells, you may start to feel symptoms. Symptoms of a cold include sneezing, sore throat, cough, headache, a mild fever, and an overall sense of discomfort. It is possible to feel cold symptoms only 10 or 12 hours after the virus is introduced into your nose. Most of the time, however, symptoms begin two or three days later.

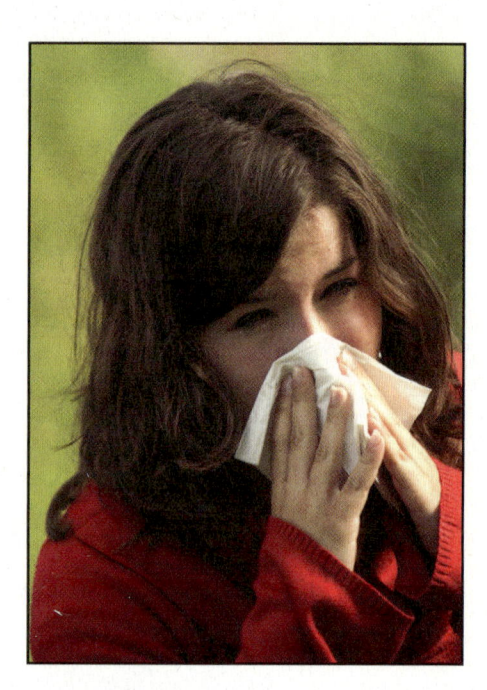

4   There are about 100 separate viruses that can cause a cold, but the most common form of the cold virus is the rhinovirus. The root word *rhino* means "nose." Most often a doctor will diagnose a cold from the symptoms. It is also possible to culture, or grow, the virus in a lab for precise identification, but there is rarely any reason to do this.

5   Cold viruses live only in the nasal passages of people and other primates, including gorillas and chimpanzees. (Yes, it is possible to give your cold to an ape!) Cold viruses grow and reproduce in the moist nasal passages. Cold viruses, though, can live for a while on surfaces such as doorknobs, hands, and computer keyboards. Most colds are contracted through person-to-person contact.

Comprehension

6 The most common way for a cold virus to spread from one person to another is through the droplets of water sprayed when a person coughs or sneezes. If a surface like a desktop or a telephone handset has been contaminated, the virus can get on your hands when you touch the contaminated surface. If you touch your face, the virus can get into your nose. It is also possible to be infected with the virus and pass it on to other people before you have any symptoms or start to feel sick.

7 You may not be able to avoid the rhinovirus altogether, but there are good habits that can protect you to some degree. Wash your hands often and well with soap and warm water; cover your mouth and nose with the inside of your elbow or a tissue when you sneeze or cough; and clean the surfaces of things that many people use, such as computer keyboards, telephones, and tables. If you think you might be coming down with a cold, avoid contact with other people. If you think someone else might be sick, keep your distance from that person until he or she feels better.

8 There isn't a lot you can do if you happen to catch a cold. Nurses, doctors, and parents will advise you to rest, keep warm, and drink a lot of liquids. There are medicines your doctor can recommend to ease your symptoms, but there is no pill that can cure the common cold. Fortunately, most colds are mild and last only for a few days or up to a week.

Comprehension

1. Why did the author most likely write this passage?
   - Ⓐ To give the reader useful health information
   - Ⓑ To entertain the reader with fascinating facts
   - Ⓒ To persuade the reader to wash his or her hands
   - Ⓓ To give the reader detailed scientific information about the rhinovirus

2. In paragraph 3, what does the word symptoms mean?
   - Ⓐ Changes indicating a disease or disorder
   - Ⓑ Feelings of sensitivity for others
   - Ⓒ Relationships between people
   - Ⓓ More than 100 different cold viruses

3. Based on this passage, what will most likely happen to the rhinovirus?
   - Ⓐ It will infect all mammals.
   - Ⓑ It will infect only people.
   - Ⓒ It will soon be wiped out.
   - Ⓓ It will continue to make people sick.

Comprehension

4. Which statement from the passage is an opinion?

    A   The most common form of cold virus is the rhinovirus.

    B   It is possible to grow the virus in a lab for precise identification.

    C   There are good habits that can protect you to some degree.

    D   If a surface like a desktop or a telephone handset has been contaminated, the virus can get on your hands.

5. What is the best way to deal with the common cold?

    A   Get a yearly vaccination.

    B   Avoid contact with cold viruses.

    C   Take medicine to kill the virus.

    D   Carry a handkerchief or tissues.

Comprehension

Directions
Read the passage. Then answer the questions that follow. Fill in the correct circle.

The Show Must Go On

1   Mr. Rosado looked at Valerie with concern. "You're telling me that two of our actors are in bed with the flu?" Mr. Rosado was the drama coach at Willard Middle School, and he also taught English.

2   "That's right, Mr. Rosado."

3   The eighth graders put on a play every year, and this year it was *Scenes from Shakespeare*. Valerie was stage manager. It was her job to make sure that the scene changes went smoothly, that the right props were on stage, and that actors were ready to make their entrances.

4   Valerie consulted the paper in her hand. Kareem was playing Romeo in the balcony scene from *Romeo and Juliet*. Jason Wong was supposed to give Marc Antony's soliloquy from *Julius Caesar*. Valerie sighed and said, "We can't do those scenes without them, and people are already going into the auditorium."

Comprehension

5 Mr. Rosado leaned back in his chair and clasped his hands in his lap. "You got the job of stage manager because you showed us you were organized and could solve problems." He sat up straight and smiled at Valerie. "Put those brains of yours to work. Surely you have some idea about what we can do."

6 Valerie thought for a minute. "I have one idea for the soliloquy."

7 "What's that?" Mr. Rosado asked.

8 "Well, Cara Cline is part of the stage crew. She's in my English class, and she recited that speech from memory when we studied *Julius Caesar*. She's about the same height as Jason so she could wear his costume."

9 "Okay, that's one problem solved. Is there another student who could play Romeo?"

10 "Maybe we don't need someone who has already memorized the part. Maybe we could get a student to stand in the shadows at the edge of the stage and read Romeo's lines from the script. Romeo is supposed to be sneaking around Juliet's home and hiding from her relatives, anyway. It would make sense that he would lurk in the shadows. I think I could get Jaime Nunez to read the part. He's selling tickets so I know he's here."

11 "You go find your actors," said Mr. Rosado. "I'll go talk to the cast and stage crew so they know what is going on. Before the program begins tonight, you can go out and announce the changes in the cast to the audience."

12 "You know what they say, don't you?" added Mr. Rosado.

13 Valerie grinned at him. "I believe they say, 'the show must go on.'"

Comprehension

6. What was probably the author's primary purpose in writing this story?

   Ⓐ Entertain the reader with an engaging story

   Ⓑ Inform the reader about theater performance

   Ⓒ Persuade the reader to become a stage manager

   Ⓓ Convince the reader to share the author's opinion

7. Under pressure, what did Valerie do?

   Ⓐ Remained calm, focused, and resourceful

   Ⓑ Became nervous, dependent, and disorganized

   Ⓒ Remained passive, observant, and responsible

   Ⓓ Became helpful, honest, and friendly

8. What lesson might the reader draw from this story?

   Ⓐ Form a committee to discuss the issues.

   Ⓑ Get the opinions of several experts.

   Ⓒ Give the job to someone more qualified.

   Ⓓ Consider a wide range of possibilities.

Comprehension

9. When do all of the events in this story happen?

    A After the performance ends
    B During the performance
    C Before the play begins
    D At the exact same time

10. How did Valerie solve the problem of two sick actors?

    A By eliminating two scenes
    B By having two actors take on a second role
    C By finding substitutes and changing one scene
    D By playing one role and having Mr. Rosario play the other

Comprehension

Directions
Read the passage. Then answer the questions that follow. Fill in the correct circle.

Your Vote Does Count!

1   Elections take place in the United States every year. Every four years, US citizens elect a president. In other years, they might vote for town officials, members of the school board, state representatives, sheriffs, or judges.

2   American citizens can register to vote when they reach the age of 18. With their votes, citizens help elect the candidate they think will do the best job. Nevertheless, many Americans who are eligible to vote do not register or do not cast their votes.

3   What does this mean? Consider the election for president of the United States in 2004. A set of pie charts below can help you understand the situation better.

4   In Chart 1, the whole pie represents the number of citizens eligible to vote in 2004. At the time of the election, about 72 percent of them were registered to vote. That is the dark blue slice of the pie chart. The remaining 28 percent shows citizens who were old enough to vote but did not register.

5   In Chart 2, the whole pie still represents the number of citizens eligible to vote in 2004. The green slice of the pie chart shows how many people actually cast votes.

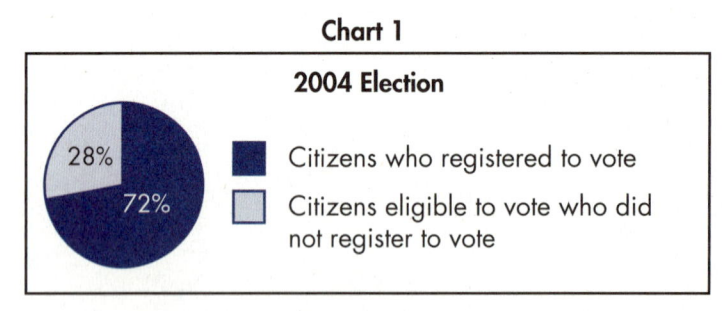

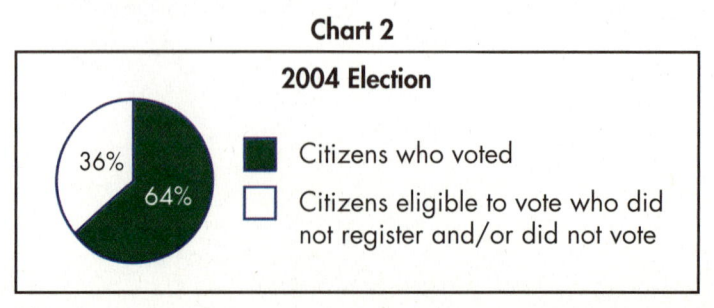

Chart 1

2004 Election

- 28% — Citizens who registered to vote
- 72% — Citizens eligible to vote who did not register to vote

Chart 2

2004 Election

- 36% — Citizens who voted
- 64% — Citizens eligible to vote who did not register and/or did not vote

Comprehension

6 Here is another way to understand the charts. Chart 1 shows that fewer than 8 out of 10 eligible people registered to vote. Chart 2 shows that fewer than 7 of 10 eligible people actually cast a vote. That means a lot of people stayed home and didn't vote. Chart 2 shows that 1 out of 3 eligible voters had no say about the outcome of the 2004 election.

7 The United States is a democracy. *Democracy* means "ruled by the people." In a perfect democracy, all the people would choose the officials who write laws, collect taxes, educate young people, and do many other things.

8 When you don't vote, it is hard to make government listen to you. Casting a vote does not mean that the man or woman you like best will always win. However, voting is the only way to make your opinions known to the people elected to government.

9 Will just one vote change the outcome of an election? It can, and it has. If one vote can make a difference, imagine what might be possible if all American citizens who are 18 or older voted in every single election!

Comprehension

11. The author of this passage probably wrote it to do what?
    - Ⓐ Persuade readers to vote
    - Ⓑ Inform readers about how to vote
    - Ⓒ Entertain readers with interesting charts
    - Ⓓ Shame readers that were eligible to vote but did not

12. What is this passage mainly about?
    - Ⓐ How to register to vote
    - Ⓑ Responsible and irresponsible citizens
    - Ⓒ The importance of registering and voting
    - Ⓓ The percentage of citizens who vote

13. How do citizens who vote compare to those who do not vote?
    - Ⓐ They write the laws of the country.
    - Ⓑ They always elect their candidates.
    - Ⓒ They keep their opinions to themselves.
    - Ⓓ They actively participate in a democracy.

Comprehension

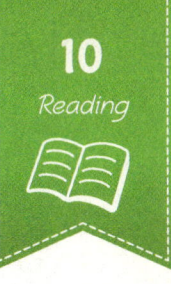

14. What is one result of voting?

    Ⓐ Your candidate always wins.

    Ⓑ Your opinions are known to elected officials.

    Ⓒ Your taxes go down.

    Ⓓ Your opinions are ignored by officials.

15. By analyzing the information in both charts, what can you conclude about those who registered to vote in 2004?

    Ⓐ 36 percent did not vote.

    Ⓑ 8 percent did not vote.

    Ⓒ 64 percent did not vote.

    Ⓓ 28 percent did not vote.

Comprehension

Directions
Read the passage. Then answer the questions that follow. Fill in the correct circle.

Rey's Cinco de Mayo Report
by Carlos Arroyo

1   When Rey thought about himself, words like *cool, smart,* and *friendly* came to mind. He might also tell you that he is an eighth grader at Sherman Oaks Middle School, a resident of Athens, New York, and a United States citizen. If you pressed him further, he might tell you which church he attended and which political party he planned to vote for when he was old enough. However, Rey rarely thought of himself as Mexican.

2   It was true that his grandparents had been born in Mexico. And his mom and dad did sometimes speak Spanish when they did not want Rey to know what they were saying. But Rey's family history did not come up too often.

3   Once in a while, a new teacher would mistakenly assume that "Rey" should be spelled *Ray,* and it was short for *Raymond.* He would politely explain that his name was spelled *Rey,* and it was short for *Reynaldo.*

4   In Rey's class, there were students who traced their family history to Europe, Asia, Africa, and South and Central America. First and foremost, they were all Americans. Rey's Mexican heritage probably would have remained at the back of his mind except that his social studies teacher, Mr. Lee, gave each student in the class an assignment to report to the class on a holiday related to the student's family background and culture.

5   Lisa Jackson was assigned to report on Juneteenth Day. This is a holiday on which African Americans celebrate the end of slavery in the United States following the Civil War. Michael Chen was given Chinese New Year. Sean Dooley would do his report on St. Patrick's Day. According to legend, the patron saint of Ireland chased all the snakes and other serpents from the island and did other good deeds.

Comprehension

6 Other students were assigned to holidays that were less well known. Eric Prekel, whose family was German, was given Oktoberfest. Rachel Stern, a Jewish girl, had the topic of Passover. Somehow, Mr. Lee found a holiday to match each student's family history. If a student's heritage was a mix of two or more cultures, Mr. Lee let the student chose a holiday from one side of the family or another.

7 Rey thought Mr. Lee would have a problem because there were two students in the class of Mexican descent. But it was no problem at all. Maria de Leon took El Dia de los Muertos (the Day of the Dead), and Rey got Cinco de Mayo.

8 At lunch, there was a lively debate about the class assignment. "I don't think a person's background is anyone's business," Brian White said. "This is America, so we are all Americans. Period. End of story."

9 "America is supposed to be 'a melting pot,'" Peter Nguyen reasoned, "but that does not mean we have to all be completely the same and give up our family histories. It is good to celebrate our diversity."

10 Rey wasn't sure how he felt. He decided to hold his judgment for a while.

11 At home that night, he told his mom and dad about it. To his surprise, they did not see eye to eye with each other. Rey's mom was very enthusiastic about his topic. "We have a mariachi costume your grandpa wore. You could bring it to school and play a recording of mariachi music!" she exclaimed. "You can interview Abuela. Your grandmother will be happy to tell you what a big deal Cinco de Mayo is in the Puebla region."

12 Rey's dad seemed to think that Rey had gotten the second-best choice. "El Dia de los Muertos, now that is a true Mexican holiday," he declared. "On that day, we honor the spirits of our relatives who have died. Cinco de Mayo is nice, too, but it is not as important," he said. That was how Rey first learned that his parents' families were from different regions of Mexico. His grandparents had met at college in Mexico City.

13 At the same time, other families around town were making similar discoveries. Rachel Stern learned that there were two dialects of Hebrew and that Jews from Eastern Europe did some things a bit differently than Jews from Spain, North Africa, and Israel. Michael Chen learned that there were many dialects of Chinese.

14 It did not take Rey long to decide that he agreed with Mr. Lee. Learning more about his own heritage and the backgrounds of his classmates was a good thing.

Comprehension

16. Based on the story, what can you decide is probably true about Rey?

   Ⓐ He did not know his grandparents came from Mexico.
   Ⓑ He wishes his name were spelled differently.
   Ⓒ He is a new student at this school.
   Ⓓ He does not speak Spanish.

17. In paragraph 11, Rey's parents do not "see eye to eye" with each other. What does the phrase see eye to eye mean?

   Ⓐ Have the same opinion about a subject
   Ⓑ Look at each other while talking
   Ⓒ Focus on the subject under discussion
   Ⓓ Examine something closely

18. Which holiday celebrates the end of slavery in the United States?

   Ⓐ Dia de los Muertos
   Ⓑ Chinese New Year
   Ⓒ Juneteenth
   Ⓓ Passover

Comprehension

19. What was the reason Mr. Lee assigned a particular holiday to each student?

    Ⓐ He wanted to pick a holiday at random out of a bag.

    Ⓑ He wanted to match the student's background and culture.

    Ⓒ He wanted everyone to do something different.

    Ⓓ He wanted to learn more about those particular holidays.

20. How do Rey's feelings about the assignment change?

    Ⓐ First he is unhappy, but later he feels it is a good thing.

    Ⓑ First he is uncertain, but later he feels it is a good thing.

    Ⓒ First he is excited, but later he feels it is a bad thing.

    Ⓓ First he is confused, but later he feels it is a bad thing.

Comprehension

Directions
Read the passage. Then answer the questions that follow. Fill in the correct circle.

Internet History

1   Everyone seems to be on the Internet these days. People do research and make personal web pages. They download music and videos. But what is the Internet? Where did it come from?

2   An *internet* is a large network made from small networks. Each small network is a group of computers that have been linked together.

3   There is also the Internet spelled with a capital *I*. It is the largest network in the world. Some people call the Internet an electronic superhighway because it can take you anywhere you want to go quickly and easily. There is a stop on the electronic superhighway where you can find out about almost anything.

4   The first electronic computers were built in the 1940s and 1950s. These huge machines filled enormous rooms. In the 1960s, scientists dreamed about ways to connect computers around the world so that they could share information. Soon they figured out what to do. The US Department of Defense developed the first network. It was called the ARPANET, which stands for "Advanced Research Projects Agency Network." Soon people who used the ARPANET began to call it the "Internet" or just "the Net."

5   This early Internet was a great success, but there were just a few people who could use it. After the invention of the personal computer, however, the Internet became more accessible to many people.

1940s–1950s: first electronic computers
↓
1960s: ARPANET
↓
1970s: first personal computers
↓
1980s: email to same ISP
↓
1990s: World Wide Web

Comprehension

6 People began to buy personal computers in the 1970s. These computers were as powerful as the early computers. They were also so small they could fit on top of a desk. Over time, there was an Internet for these personal computers, too. All you needed was an "Internet Service Provider," or ISP. Each ISP offered a service called email. At first, you could send email only to people who used the same ISP. In the early 1990s, though, researchers at the CERN, a laboratory in Europe, developed the World Wide Web. This information system integrates graphics and hypertext and allows users easy, universal access to each other and to information around the world.

7 In 1995, the Federal Networking Council of the United States wrote an official definition of the Internet. That was the first step toward turning the Internet into big business. Access to the Internet was turned over to the ISPs. Competition among the ISPs has helped the Internet grow. To attract customers, ISP companies have made it easier to search for websites. They also offer new and better services to people who want to navigate the electronic superhighway.

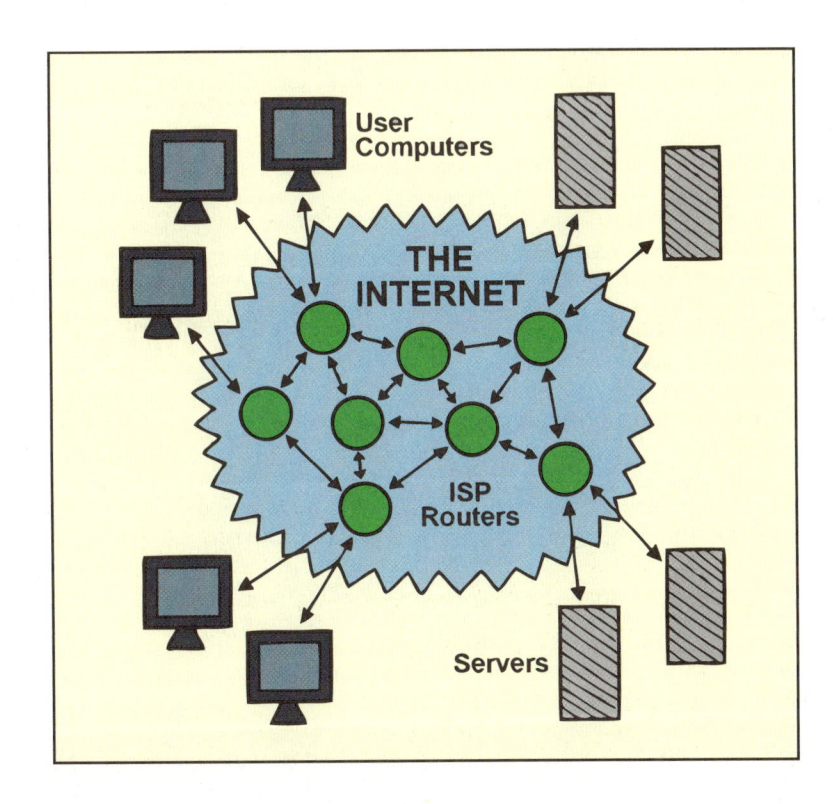

Comprehension

21. What does the rapid development of the Internet suggest?

    Ⓐ The technology required was simple.

    Ⓑ There was a need for speedy world-wide communication.

    Ⓒ People were satisfied with the first email technology.

    Ⓓ Only scientists had an interest in communicating through computers.

22. What does the word <u>network</u> mean in paragraph 2?

    Ⓐ A group of people

    Ⓑ A structure of wires that cross

    Ⓒ A system of connected computers

    Ⓓ A group of radio or television stations

23. How was ARPANET different from the later electronic superhighway?

    Ⓐ It was unsuccessful.

    Ⓑ It was only used for business.

    Ⓒ It was not available to many people.

    Ⓓ It was available in the 1940s and 1950s.

Comprehension

24. Based on this passage, what will probably be true of the Internet in the near future?

    Ⓐ It will be replaced.

    Ⓑ It will eliminate all need for travel.

    Ⓒ It will have the same number of users.

    Ⓓ It will be used by most people.

25. To create the Internet, what was the main problem that had to be solved?

    Ⓐ Making up for the lack of small computers

    Ⓑ Laying communication wires across oceans

    Ⓒ Deciding whether to use English or another language

    Ⓓ Connecting many computers in one electronic network

Comprehension

Directions
Read the poem. Then answer the questions that follow. Fill in the correct circle.

Les Silhouettes
by Oscar Wilde

1   The sea is flecked with bars of grey
    The dull dead wind is out of tune,
    And like a withered leaf the moon
Is blown across the stormy bay.

2   Etched clear upon the pallid sand
    The black boat lies: a sailor boy
    Clambers aboard in careless joy
With laughing face and gleaming hand.

3   And overhead the curlews cry,
    Where through the dusky upland grass
    The young brown-throated reapers pass,
Like silhouettes against the sky.

Comprehension

26. What is the rhyming pattern in stanza 1?

    (A) AABB

    (B) ABAB

    (C) ABBA

    (D) ABCD

27. In contrast to the words *grey, dull, dead,* and *withered* in stanza 1, the words *clear, joy, laughing,* and *gleaming* in stanza 2 express what change in mood?

    (A) From happy to sad

    (B) From gloomy to hopeful

    (C) From bitter to forgiving

    (D) From kind to hateful

28. Based on the images in this poem, what else did the author likely write?

    (A) Mostly romantic stories

    (B) Mystery stories about the sea

    (C) Other poems about the seacoast

    (D) Nonfiction articles about weather

Comprehension

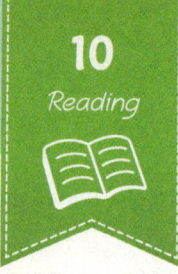

29. What are the colors of the images described in this poem?

- Ⓐ Multi-colored
- Ⓑ Light pastel colors
- Ⓒ Black, white, and grey
- Ⓓ Mostly pale blue sky and grey sea

30. What is the meaning of the word <u>bars</u> in stanza 1?

- Ⓐ Stripes
- Ⓑ Obstructions
- Ⓒ Courtroom railings
- Ⓓ Long, thin pieces of metal

Unit 4 WRITING

LESSON 11
Standard 1

Mechanics and Structure 1
- read a question
- read four answer choices
- fill in the correct answer to the question

LESSON 12
Standard 1

Mechanics and Structure 2
- read a question
- read four answer choices
- fill in the correct answer to the question

LESSON 13
Standards 1, 2

Descriptive Writing Paragraph
- look at a picture
- write a paragraph that describes the picture
- use a checklist to check your writing

LESSON 14
Standard 3

Fact-Based Essay
- read a text prompt and look at a chart, map, table, or other graphic
- write an essay using the prompt and graphic
- use a checklist to check your writing

LESSON 11 Writing

Mechanics and Structure 1

Directions
Read the question and answers. Fill in the correct circle.

1. Which sentence is correct?
   - Ⓐ They's here.
   - Ⓑ There here.
   - Ⓒ They're here.
   - Ⓓ Their here.

2. Which sentence is correct?
   - Ⓐ He brushes all his tooths twice a day.
   - Ⓑ He brushes all his teeth twice a day.
   - Ⓒ He brush all his teethes twice a day.
   - Ⓓ He brush all his teeths twice a day.

3. Which sentence is correct?
   - Ⓐ The student tries to do her best in school.
   - Ⓑ The student try to do her best in school.
   - Ⓒ The students try to do her best in school.
   - Ⓓ The students tries to do her best in school.

Mechanics and Structure 1

Directions
Read the question and answers. Fill in the correct circle.

4. Which sentence is correct?
   - Ⓐ Did they knew what to do?
   - Ⓑ Did know they what to do.
   - Ⓒ Did they know what to do?
   - Ⓓ Did know what to do.

5. Which sentence is correct?
   - Ⓐ The tree fall during the storm.
   - Ⓑ The tree fell during the storm.
   - Ⓒ The tree falled during the storm.
   - Ⓓ The tree fallen during the storm.

6. Which sentence is correct?
   - Ⓐ Those books are our.
   - Ⓑ Those books are hours.
   - Ⓒ Those books are our's.
   - Ⓓ Those books are ours.

Mechanics and Structure 1

Directions
Read the question and answers. Fill in the correct circle.

7. Which sentence is correct?
   - Ⓐ They are doing well, thanks.
   - Ⓑ They is doing well, thanks.
   - Ⓒ They's doing well, thanks.
   - Ⓓ They doing well, thanks.

8. Which sentence is correct?
   - Ⓐ Where is Mr. Smith's hat?
   - Ⓑ Where is mr. smith's hat?
   - Ⓒ Where is Mr Smiths hat?
   - Ⓓ Where is Mr. Smith hat?

9. Which sentence is correct?
   - Ⓐ The dog licked is bowl clean.
   - Ⓑ The dog licked it's bowl clean.
   - Ⓒ The dog licked its bowl clean.
   - Ⓓ The dog licked its' bowl clean.

Mechanics and Structure 1

Directions
Read the question and answers. Fill in the correct circle.

10. Which sentence is correct?
    - Ⓐ They flew to Mexico in may.
    - Ⓑ They flew to Mexico in May.
    - Ⓒ They had fly to Mexico in may.
    - Ⓓ They had flowned to mexico in May.

11. Which sentence is correct?
    - Ⓐ Please sit next to I.
    - Ⓑ Please sit next me.
    - Ⓒ Please sit to me next.
    - Ⓓ Please sit next to me.

12. Which sentence is correct?
    - Ⓐ We leaving for the airport soon.
    - Ⓑ Were leaving for the airport soon.
    - Ⓒ We're leaving for the airport soon.
    - Ⓓ Were leave for the airport soon.

LESSON 12

Mechanics and Structure 2

Directions
Read the sentence and look at the underlined part. If there is a mistake, choose the correct answer. If there is no mistake, choose *Correct as is*. Fill in the correct circle.

1. The students <u>have become</u> good writers.

   Which answer is correct?

   Ⓐ become
   Ⓑ becoming
   Ⓒ has become
   Ⓓ Correct as is

2. The artist uses <u>a lotta</u> paint.

   Which answer is correct?

   Ⓐ lotsa
   Ⓑ a lot of
   Ⓒ a lot
   Ⓓ Correct as is

3. The girl <u>will comes</u> to science class.

   Which answer is correct?

   Ⓐ will came
   Ⓑ will coming
   Ⓒ will come
   Ⓓ Correct as is

Mechanics and Structure 2

Directions
Read the sentence and look at the underlined part. If there is a mistake, choose the correct answer. If there is no mistake, choose *Correct as is*. Fill in the correct circle.

4. <u>Its four oclock</u> now.

    Which answer is correct?

    - Ⓐ Its four o'clock
    - Ⓑ It's four oclock
    - Ⓒ It's four o'clock
    - Ⓓ Correct as is

5. Give <u>they</u> the tickets to the concert.

    Which answer is correct?

    - Ⓐ their
    - Ⓑ them
    - Ⓒ thems
    - Ⓓ Correct as is

6. The runner ran <u>more rapid</u> than ever before.

    Which answer is correct?

    - Ⓐ rapider
    - Ⓑ more rapider
    - Ⓒ more rapidly
    - Ⓓ Correct as is

12 Writing

Mechanics and Structure 2

Directions
Read the sentence and look at the underlined part. If there is a mistake, choose the correct answer. If there is no mistake, choose *Correct as is*. Fill in the correct circle.

7. Many people like to watch <u>mens'</u> soccer on television.

   Which answer is correct?

   - Ⓐ men's
   - Ⓑ man's
   - Ⓒ men
   - Ⓓ Correct as is

8. She lives on <u>North Market Street</u>.

   Which answer is correct?

   - Ⓐ north market street
   - Ⓑ north Market Street
   - Ⓒ North Market street
   - Ⓓ Correct as is

9. The red car is <u>her</u>.

   Which answer is correct?

   - Ⓐ hers
   - Ⓑ her's
   - Ⓒ she's
   - Ⓓ Correct as is

Mechanics and Structure 2

Directions
Read the sentence and look at the underlined part. If there is a mistake, choose the correct answer. If there is no mistake, choose *Correct as is*. Fill in the correct circle.

10. <u>Have they wrote</u> their research reports yet?

    Which answer is correct?

    - (A) Have they writen
    - (B) Have they written
    - (C) Has they wrote
    - (D) Correct as is

11. How many <u>childs</u> are in kindergarten?

    Which answer is correct?

    - (A) childern
    - (B) children
    - (C) child
    - (D) Correct as is

12. We <u>is not going</u> to the picnic on Saturday.

    Which answer is correct?

    - (A) is not go
    - (B) are not going
    - (C) are not go
    - (D) Correct as is

LESSON 13 Writing

Descriptive Writing Paragraph

Directions
Write a paragraph that describes what is happening in the picture. Include as many details as you can. Someone who reads your paragraph should be able to imagine the entire scene.

Look at the picture carefully and think about:

- What is the time and place?
- Who is the person, and what is he doing?
- What might the person be thinking or feeling?

1.

GO ON

Descriptive Writing Paragraph

1.

✓ Check Your Work

- ☐ Write one paragraph.
- ☐ Write a topic sentence.
- ☐ Use details in your writing.
- ☐ Write complete sentences.
- ☐ Write a concluding sentence.
- ☐ Use correct capitalization, punctuation, and spelling.

STOP

Descriptive Writing Paragraph

Directions

Write a paragraph that describes what is happening in the picture. Include as many details as you can. Someone who reads your paragraph should be able to imagine the entire scene.

Look at the picture carefully and think about:

- What is the time and place?
- Who are the people, and what are they doing?
- What might the people be thinking or feeling?

2.

Descriptive Writing Paragraph

2.

✓ Check Your Work

- ☐ Write one paragraph.
- ☐ Write a topic sentence.
- ☐ Use details in your writing.
- ☐ Write complete sentences.
- ☐ Write a concluding sentence.
- ☐ Use correct capitalization, punctuation, and spelling.

STOP

13 Writing

Descriptive Writing Paragraph

Directions
Write a paragraph that describes what is happening in the picture. Include as many details as you can. Someone who reads your paragraph should be able to imagine the entire scene.

Look at the picture carefully and think about:

- What is the time and place?
- Who is the person, and what is she doing?
- What might the person be thinking or feeling?

3.

Descriptive Writing Paragraph

3.

> ✓ **Check Your Work**
>
> ☐ Write one paragraph.
> ☐ Write a topic sentence.
> ☐ Use details in your writing.
> ☐ Write complete sentences.
> ☐ Write a concluding sentence.
> ☐ Use correct capitalization, punctuation, and spelling.

STOP

13 Writing

Descriptive Writing Paragraph

Directions
Write a paragraph that describes what is happening in the picture. Include as many details as you can. Someone who reads your paragraph should be able to imagine the entire scene.

Look at the picture carefully and think about:

- What is the time and place?
- Who are the people, and what are they doing?
- What might the people be thinking or feeling?

4.

Descriptive Writing Paragraph

4.

✓ Check Your Work

- ☐ Write one paragraph.
- ☐ Write a topic sentence.
- ☐ Use details in your writing.
- ☐ Write complete sentences.
- ☐ Write a concluding sentence.
- ☐ Use correct capitalization, punctuation, and spelling.

STOP

13 Writing

Descriptive Writing Paragraph

Directions
Write a paragraph that describes what is happening in the picture. Include as many details as you can. Someone who reads your paragraph should be able to imagine the entire scene.

Look at the picture carefully and think about:

- What is the time and place?
- Who is the person, and what is he doing?
- What might the person be thinking or feeling?

5.

GO ON

Descriptive Writing Paragraph

5.

_____
_____
_____
_____
_____

> ☑ **Check Your Work**
>
> ☐ Write one paragraph.
> ☐ Write a topic sentence.
> ☐ Use details in your writing.
> ☐ Write complete sentences.
> ☐ Write a concluding sentence.
> ☐ Use correct capitalization, punctuation, and spelling.

_____
_____
_____
_____
_____
_____
_____
_____
_____
_____

STOP

Fact-Based Essay

LESSON 14 Writing

Directions
Look at the map and chart. They show information about two American colonies. Imagine it is 1720 and you are going to move to one of these colonies. Which would you choose, Massachusetts or Pennsylvania?

In your own words, write a well-organized essay about the place you would rather live. Use information from both the map and the chart to support your essay.

Remember to include:

- an introduction, body, and conclusion.
- information from the map and chart.
- details, examples, or reasons.

You may include other information you know about the topic.

1.

Fact–Based Essay

1.

TWO AMERICAN COLONIES IN 1720

	Massachusetts	Pennsylvania
Location	New England	Mid-Atlantic
Founded	1630	1682
Founder	John Winthrop	William Penn
Population in 1720	91,000	31,000
Reasons for Founding	Religious freedom for Puritans Commercial profit	Religious freedom for Quakers, Catholics, Jews, and others Commercial profit
Freedom of Religion?	No	Yes
Where Settlers Came From	England	England, Switzerland, Germany, Netherlands, and other countries
Climate	Short, cool summers Long, extremely cold winters	Average warm summers Average cool winters
Geography	Poor, rocky soil; rugged seacoast; mountains, marshes	Rich soil; rolling hills; protected river valleys, mountains
Natural Resources	Fish, whales, timber	Rich farmland, timber, iron ore, coal
Economy	Fishing, whaling, logging, shipbuilding, shipping and trade	Farming, especially wheat and corn; mining; lumber; textiles, iron manufacturing
People Mostly Live in—	Cities and towns	Small towns and farms
Major Town	Boston	Philadelphia

GO ON ➡

UNIT 4 Writing

Fact-Based Essay

Plan Your Answer

You may use this space to plan your answer for question 1. Read the question and make notes below about how you might answer it. Do **not** write your final answer on this page. Your writing on this page will **not** be scored. Write your final answer on pages 131–132.

Fact-Based Essay

1.

✓ Check Your Work

- ☐ Write about the topic.
- ☐ Include an introduction, body, and conclusion.
- ☐ Use details, examples, or reasons in your writing.
- ☐ Write complete sentences and paragraphs.
- ☐ Use correct grammar, punctuation, and spelling.

GO ON ➡

Fact-Based Essay

Fact-Based Essay

Directions
Look at the diagram and the table. The diagram shows the arrangement of planets in the solar system. The table lists the length of a day and a year on each planet, in Earth time.

In your own words, write a well-organized essay comparing the day and year length on other planets to a day and year on Earth. Use information from both the diagram and the table to support your essay.

Remember to include:

- an introduction, body, and conclusion.
- information from the diagram and table.
- details, examples, or reasons.

You may include other information you know about the topic.

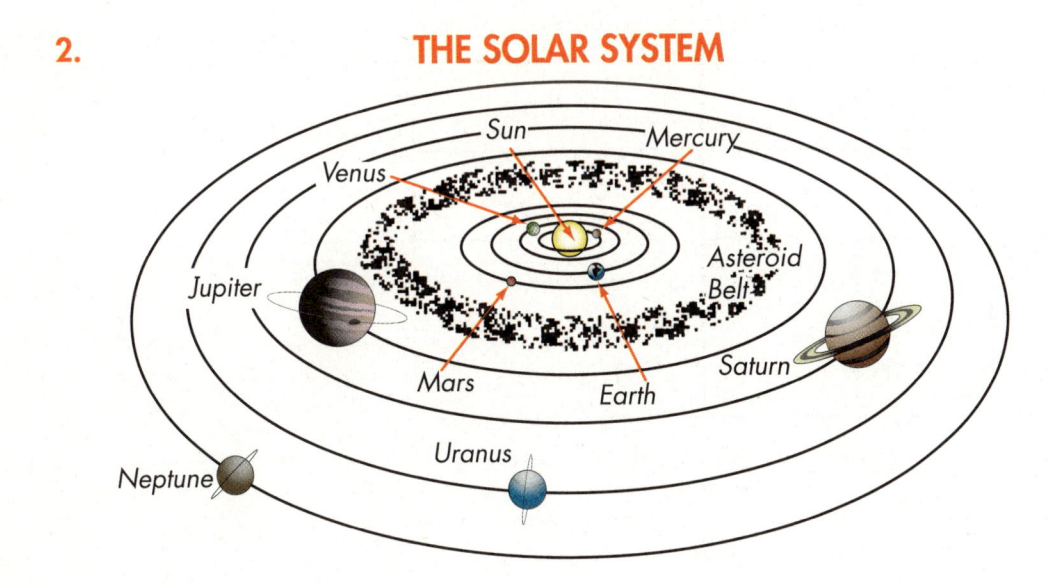

2.

THE SOLAR SYSTEM

Fact-Based Essay

2. **PLANETS OF THE SOLAR SYSTEM: DAY AND YEAR LENGTH**

Planet	Rotation (Length of a Day in Earth Time)*	Revolution (Length of a Year in Earth Time)*
Mercury	59 days	3 months
Venus	243 days	7.5 months
Earth	1 day	1 year
Mars	1 day	1.9 years
Jupiter	10 hours	12 years
Saturn	11 hours	29.5 years
Uranus	17 hours	84 years
Neptune	16 hours	165 years

*These are approximations.

GO ON

Fact-Based Essay

Plan Your Answer

You may use this space to plan your answer for question 2. Read the question and make notes below about how you might answer it. Do **not** write your final answer on this page. Your writing on this page will **not** be scored. Write your final answer on pages 136–137.

Fact-Based Essay

2.

✓ Check Your Work

☐ Write about the topic.
☐ Include an introduction, body, and conclusion.
☐ Use details, examples, or reasons in your writing.
☐ Write complete sentences and paragraphs.
☐ Use correct grammar, punctuation, and spelling.

GO ON ➡

Fact-Based Essay

14 Writing

Fact-Based Essay

Directions

Look at the diagram and table. The diagram shows the process for recycling plastic. The table shows information about different kinds of plastics.

In your own words, write a well-organized essay about recycling plastics. Describe where different kinds of plastics come from, how they are processed, and what kinds of products they become. Use information from both the diagram and table to support your essay.

Remember to include:

- an introduction, body, and conclusion.
- information from the diagram and table.
- details, examples, or reasons.

You may include other information you know about the topic.

3.

PLASTICS RECYCLING PROCESS

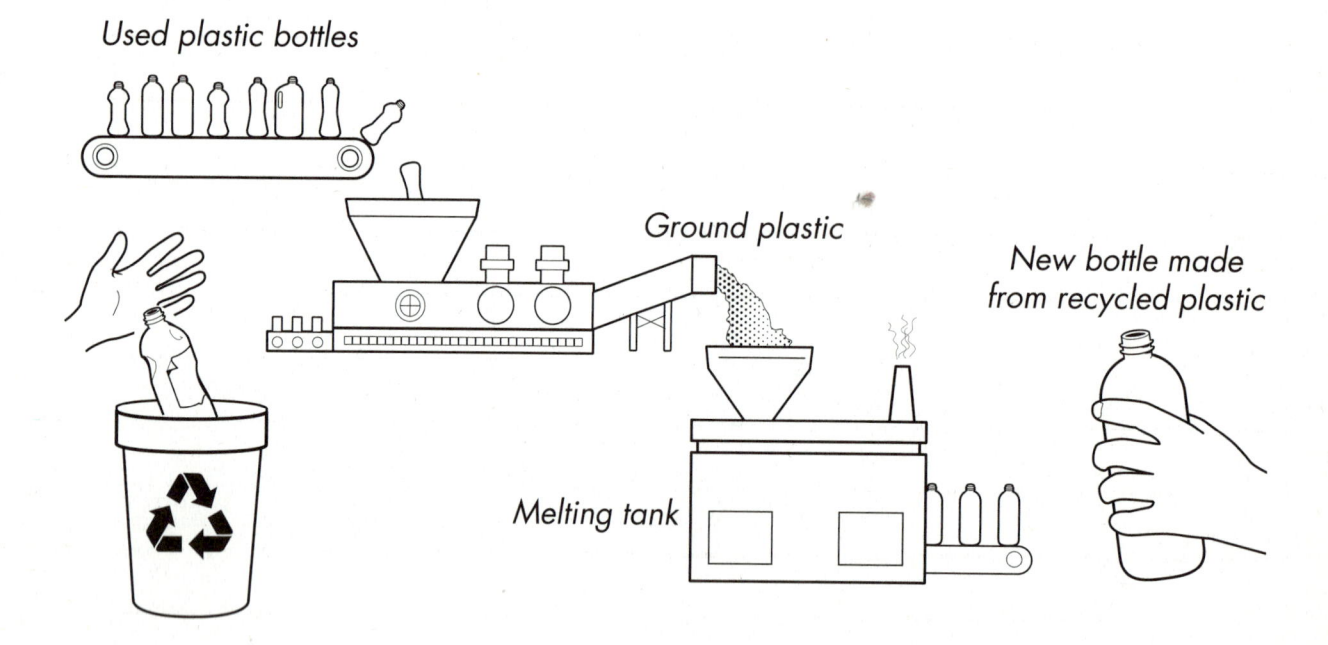

Used plastic bottles

Ground plastic

New bottle made from recycled plastic

Melting tank

GO ON →

138 UNIT 4 Writing

Fact-Based Essay

3. **RECYCLING PLASTICS**

Number and Abbreviation	Some Things It Is Found In	Some Things It Is Recycled Into
1 PET or PETE	Water and soft drink bottles	Thread and yarn for textiles such as clothing and carpet
2 HDPE	Milk jugs Bleach and detergent bottles	Laundry detergent bottles Lumber Picnic tables
3 PVC	Shampoo bottles Pipes	Flooring Deck lumber
4 LDPE	Squeeze bottles Shopping bags	Trash can liners Floor tiles
5 PP	Yogurt containers Medicine bottles	Tool handles (brooms, brushes, etc.) Trays
6 PS	Disposable cups and food containers CD cases	Insulation Foam packing peanuts
7 Others	5-gallon water jugs Computer cases	Plastic lumber

GO ON →

Fact–Based Essay

Plan Your Answer

You may use this space to plan your answer for question 3. Read the question and make notes below about how you might answer it. Do **not** write your final answer on this page. Your writing on this page will **not** be scored. Write your final answer on pages 141–142.

GO ON

Fact-Based Essay

3.

✓ Check Your Work

- ☐ Write about the topic.
- ☐ Include an introduction, body, and conclusion.
- ☐ Use details, examples, or reasons in your writing.
- ☐ Write complete sentences and paragraphs.
- ☐ Use correct grammar, punctuation, and spelling.

GO ON ➡

14 Fact-Based Essay

Fact-Based Essay

Directions

Look at the flyers on this page and the next. They describe two volunteer jobs. They tell what the volunteers will be doing and the job requirements. Which of these jobs would you prefer to volunteer for?

In your own words, write a well-organized essay about the volunteer job you would prefer. Explain why you think you could do that job and why it appeals to you. Use information from the flyers to support your essay.

Remember to include:

- an introduction, body, and conclusion.
- information from the flyers.
- details, examples, or reasons.

You may include other information you know about the topic.

4.

VOLUNTEER JOB: STREAM CLEANUP

What?	Help clean up a local stream: • Remove trash from stream • Pick up litter from stream banks • Clean out bird nesting boxes • Pull up invasive plants
Where?	Bent Creek in Springville Park
When?	Earth Day April 22 from 8 A.M. to 2 P.M. Rain or shine!
Who?	Anyone age 12 and up
We'll Provide	• Work gloves • Tools • Trash bags • Drinking water
You'll Need	• Old clothes and shoes • Sunglasses and a hat • Sunblock • A snack to eat

If you don't mind getting wet and dirty, this is the job for you!

GO ON ➡

14 Writing: Fact–Based Essay

4.

VOLUNTEER JOB: LIBRARY BOOK SALE

What?	Help prepare for the annual library book sale
	December to April: • collect books from donation bins • sort books, CDs, and DVDs by type • box donations • keep records
	During the April sale: • unload boxes onto tables by category • keep tables stocked • help people find categories • work the checkout and make change • bag books for customers • help customers carry books to cars
Where?	Springville Library
When?	December to April: • Thursday evenings from 4 P.M. to 8 P.M. • Saturdays from 8 A.M. to 4 P.M.
	Book Sale: • April 26 set-up from noon to ? • April 27 sale from 8 A.M. to 5 P.M.
Who?	Anyone age 12 and up—we'll find a job for you!
We'll Provide	• Boxes • Markers • Friendly faces!
You'll Need	• Enthusiasm! • Strong back • Ability to do math and make change

If you love books, you'll love helping us with the Annual Book Lovers' Sale!

GO ON ➡

Fact-Based Essay

Plan Your Answer

You may use this space to plan your answer for question 4. Read the question and make notes below about how you might answer it. Do **not** write your final answer on this page. Your writing on this page will **not** be scored. Write your final answer on pages 146–147.

14 Writing

Fact-Based Essay

4. _____

✓ Check Your Work

- ☐ Write about the topic.
- ☐ Include an introduction, body, and conclusion.
- ☐ Use details, examples, or reasons in your writing.
- ☐ Write complete sentences and paragraphs.
- ☐ Use correct grammar, punctuation, and spelling.

GO ON ➡

Fact-Based Essay

14 Writing

Fact-Based Essay

Directions
Look at the time lines. They show events in the lives of two important women scientists, Sally Ride and Sylvia Earle.

In your own words, write a well-organized essay about one of these women. Describe why that woman was important and what contributions she made to her field of science. Use information from the time lines to support your essay.

Remember to include:

- an introduction, body, and conclusion.
- information from the time lines.
- details, examples, or reasons.

You may include other information you know about the topic.

5.
TIME LINE OF EVENTS FOR SALLY RIDE

1951	Born in Los Angeles, California. As a child, she enjoys looking through telescopes at the stars and planets.
1968	Graduates from high school, where her favorite subjects were math and science
1973	Graduates from Stanford University with degrees in English and physics
1975	Earns a masters degree in science
1978	Becomes Dr. Sally Ride when she gets her doctorate in science from Stanford University. In that year, she becomes an astronaut for NASA.
1982	Chosen to be the first American woman in space
1983	Flies into space for the first time as a member of the *Challenger* space shuttle crew. The *Challenger* launches from Kennedy Space Center in Florida and it orbits Earth for six days. On this flight, she is the first to use a robot arm to retrieve a satellite.
1984	Flies into space for the second time with four other astronauts and two scientists
1986	Her third flight into space is cancelled after the *Challenger* space shuttle explodes during a launch. The accident kills all of the astronauts on board. Dr. Ride is assigned to help find the cause of the accident.
1989	Begins teaching physics at the University of California in San Diego. Writes *To Space and Back*, about her experiences as an astronaut.
2001	Starts a company to help young girls learn science. As the company president, she serves as a role model for girls who want to study science.
2003	Appointed to the committee to help find the cause of a second space shuttle disaster
2012	Dies in California at the age of 61

GO ON ➡

Fact-Based Essay

5.   **TIME LINE OF EVENTS FOR SYLVIA EARLE**

1935	Born in Gibbstown, New Jersey
1948	Moves to Clearwater, Florida, where she falls in love with the ocean
1955	Graduates from Florida State University, where she learns to scuba dive
1956	Earns a masters degree in science from Duke University
1964	Joins a six-week ocean National Science Foundation research trip to the Indian Ocean, the first of many research projects over the years
1966	Becomes Dr. Earle when she gets her doctorate in oceanography from Duke University
1968	Becomes first person to dive 100 feet down in the submersible ship *Deep Diver*
1970	Leads the Tektite Project, in which she lives with four other women in an undersea home for two weeks
1979	Walks on the sea floor, at a depth of 1250 feet in a pressurized suit, unconnected to the surface. Also sets a record for solo diving in a submersible at a depth of 3,300 feet.
1980	Writes *Exploring the Deep Frontier,* about her experiences in the depths of the ocean. Begins serving on the National Advisory Committee on Oceans and Atmosphere.
1982	Starts a company, Deep Ocean Engineering, to design and build deep-sea exploration subs
1985	Starts a second company, Deep Ocean Technologies, which builds the *Deep Rover* research submarine
1990	Appointed Chief Scientist at NOAA (National Oceanographic and Atmospheric Administration)
1992	Starts a third company, Deep Ocean Exploration & Research
1998	Is named an Explorer in Residence by the National Geographic Society
2009	Receives a TED award for her work to save the world's oceans
2010	Serves as a consultant for the *Deepwater Horizon* oil spill
2012	Leads expedition to the NOAA's Aquarius underwater laboratory

GO ON

Fact-Based Essay

Plan Your Answer

You may use this space to plan your answer for question 5. Read the question and make notes below about how you might answer it. Do **not** write your final answer on this page. Your writing on this page will **not** be scored. Write your final answer on pages 151–152.

Fact-Based Essay

5.

✓ Check Your Work

- ☐ Write about the topic.
- ☐ Include an introduction, body, and conclusion.
- ☐ Use details, examples, or reasons in your writing.
- ☐ Write complete sentences and paragraphs.
- ☐ Use correct grammar, punctuation, and spelling.

GO ON ➡

Fact-Based Essay

Unit 5
TRANSITION to ELA

SESSION 1
*Standards
RI.1–5, 9*

Informational
- read an informational passage
- read questions about the passage
- fill in the correct answers to the multiple-choice questions
- write answers to the short-response questions

SESSION 2
*Standards
RL.1–5*

Literary
- read a literary passage
- read questions about the passage
- fill in the correct answers to the multiple-choice questions
- write answers to the short-response questions

SESSION 1

Informational

In Session 1, you will read two informational passages:
- Preparing to Be Weightless
- Herman Melville

There are multiple-choice and short written response questions for you to answer after each passage. Read the passages as often as you need to. Then answer the questions. Keep working until you see the word STOP at the bottom of page 164.

Informational

Directions
Read the passage and answer questions 1 through 7.

Preparing to Be Weightless

1   When astronauts spend time at the International Space Station, they have to live and work in an environment where they are weightless. Weight is one expression of gravity. There is so little gravity in space it is called "microgravity."

2   Gravity is the force that draws objects toward each other. Gravity is everywhere, but larger objects exert a stronger gravitational pull than smaller objects.

3   The moon, for example, is much smaller than Earth. Gravity on the moon is about one-sixth what it is on Earth. In other words, a person who weighs 120 pounds on Earth would weigh about 20 pounds on the moon. Jupiter is the largest planet in our solar system, and gravity there is two-and-a-half times what it is on Earth. A person who weighs 120 pounds on Earth would weigh 300 pounds on Jupiter! In space, far away from any planet, there seems to be no gravity at all. Without gravity, astronauts—and everything around them—float.

4   Astronauts have to practice moving, working, eating, and sleeping in microgravity. Most of their training takes place in a large swimming pool in the "neutral buoyancy laboratory," or NBL.

5   "Neutral buoyancy" means that an object neither floats nor sinks. Imagine tossing a stone or a stick into a lake or pond. The stone sinks right to the bottom, but the stick floats on the surface of the water. An object with neutral buoyancy would be suspended somewhere in the middle.

6   Astronauts achieve neutral buoyancy in the pool by wearing a special suit. They can position themselves as though they were lying down, as well as standing up.

GO ON

Informational

7   The NBL provides good training for work in outer space, but it is not a weightless environment. The astronauts inside the suits still feel their own weight. In addition, as the astronauts move in the water, the water "drags" against their arms and tools. Imagine wading through water to get a sense of how that feels.

8   In fact, it is very difficult to create an environment of weightlessness, or microgravity, on Earth. Microgravity can be achieved in a special aircraft for only about 20 seconds at a time.

9   These special aircraft fly in a curving pattern up and down. This pattern is called a parabola, which is a curve just like the arc of a baseball through the air.

10   At first, the aircraft must climb and accelerate strongly. When it is going fast enough, the pilot reduces the engine power to nearly zero. When this happens, the speed of the plane moving upward is almost equal to the force of gravity pulling it downward. The effect inside the plane is a period of microgravity that lasts for about 20 seconds. Then, as the plane begins to slow, gravity pulls it back toward Earth. At this point, the pilot increases engine power and brings the plane back onto a "flat" flight path. A moment later, the plane will accelerate and climb, and the astronauts will prepare to experience another 20 seconds of microgravity.

1. What is this passage mainly about?
   - (A) How the neutral buoyancy laboratory works
   - (B) How microgravity is created in an aircraft
   - (C) How gravity behaves on Earth, the moon, and Jupiter
   - (D) How astronauts prepare for working in microgravity

GO ON ➡

Informational

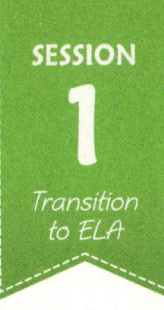

SESSION 1
Transition to ELA

2. What problem in astronaut training is solved by using special aircraft?

- Ⓐ Fitting astronauts in special suits
- Ⓑ Teaching astronauts how to float
- Ⓒ Making a neutral buoyancy environment
- Ⓓ Creating a microgravity environment on Earth

3. How does gravity on Earth compare to gravity on the moon and Jupiter?

- Ⓐ It is the same as the moon and Jupiter.
- Ⓑ It is greater than Jupiter and less than the moon.
- Ⓒ It is greater than the moon and less than Jupiter.
- Ⓓ It is the same as Jupiter and more than the moon.

4. At the NBL, what causes the effect of neutral buoyancy?

- Ⓐ A special suit that trainees wear
- Ⓑ Altering the density of the water
- Ⓒ Wading through the water
- Ⓓ Changing positions from "standing up" to "lying down"

GO ON ➡

SESSION 1 Transition to ELA

Informational

5. Based on information in the passage, why do you think scientists spend so much time and effort to simulate microgravity on Earth?

   Ⓐ Microgravity environments help to understand Earth's past.

   Ⓑ Astronauts have to be ready to work when they go into space.

   Ⓒ There will be future business opportunities in microgravity environments.

   Ⓓ In the future, gravity on Earth may decrease, and scientists will be ready.

6. What is a parabola and how is it related to achieving microgravity? Use details from the passage to support your answer.

   Write your answer in complete sentences.

   _____
   _____
   _____
   _____
   _____
   _____
   _____

   GO ON ➡

Informational

7. Which training experience, the NBL or the special aircraft, probably gives the astronauts a truer sense of the weightlessness they will have on the International Space Station? Why? Use details from the passage to support your answer.

Write your answer in complete sentences.

_____
_____
_____
_____
_____
_____
_____

Informational

Directions
Read the passage and answer questions 8 through 14.

Herman Melville
by Richard Masters

1   Whales fascinate people. It is easy to understand why. These giant marine mammals are amazing when they swim in the ocean. How can something so huge maneuver so gracefully? A closer view of a whale in an aquarium or aquatic theme park only adds to the impression that this animal is special. One look in the eyes of a whale and you will come away convinced that they are as intelligent as they are huge!

2   The most famous book about whales was written in 1851. *Moby Dick,* by Herman Melville, is a marvelous classic of American literature. Melville created this work of fiction using some of his own life experiences.

3   Herman Melville was born in New York City on August 1, 1819. His prosperous family had made their money as merchants. When he was a small child, Melville listened as his father told tales of adventures at sea. Although his father died when Melville was young and the family moved to a small town, the tales he had heard as a child seemed to have a lasting effect on him.

4   After Melville finished school, he worked briefly on his uncle's farm. Soon, however, he quit that job and signed on as a cabin boy on a merchant ship. In 1841, Melville secured a position on a whaling ship bound for the Pacific Ocean. For the next three years, he served on several ships. He interrupted his life at sea a few times for adventures on Pacific islands.

GO ON

Informational

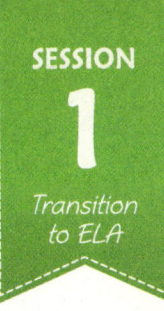

5   These adventures would provide Melville with material for many of his books. When he returned to New York, Melville began writing novels, stories, and poetry. His first two books, *Typee* and *Omoo,* were based on his adventures and were very successful. *Moby Dick* is by far the best known of his works today, and it is considered his masterpiece. When it was published in 1851, however, it did not do very well either with the public or with critics.

6   *Moby Dick* is the story of a whaling voyage during which the captain, Ahab, is searching for the great white whale, Moby Dick. The two had an earlier encounter. As a result, the captain lost his leg. Told from the point of view of a seaman named Ishmael, the tale is famous for its gripping story as well as its detail and lengthy descriptions of all aspects of whaling. The book combines the adventure story with musings on the meaning of life and other philosophical questions. The captain has an obsession with finding the whale that cost him his leg. The plot of the story has been examined closely by generations of literary critics.

7   Melville married Elizabeth Shaw, the daughter of a prominent family, in 1847. They had four children and lived in rural Massachusetts. Eventually, he and his family moved to New York City, where he got a job with a customs house. It was this position that enabled him to support his family, though he continued to write. However, his work never regained great popularity in his lifetime. Melville died on September 28, 1891.

8   Today, most critics of literature consider *Moby Dick* one of the great American novels. There are even college courses that spend an entire semester studying this one book.

8. How did Herman Melville find background information for his book about whaling?

    (A) He interviewed sailors and whalers.

    (B) He actually worked on a whaling ship.

    (C) He read books on the topic by other authors.

    (D) He watched whalers when he lived on a Pacific island.

GO ON

SESSION 1 — Transition to ELA

Informational

9. What is the meaning of the word <u>maneuver</u> in paragraph 1?

- Ⓐ Eat
- Ⓑ Dress
- Ⓒ Speak
- Ⓓ Move

10. From information in the passage, what can you tell about Herman Melville?

- Ⓐ He was very athletic.
- Ⓑ He was very sociable.
- Ⓒ He was very generous.
- Ⓓ He was very adventurous.

11. Based on information in the passage, readers can tell that the character of Captain Ahab was motivated by a desire for what?

- Ⓐ Love
- Ⓑ Justice
- Ⓒ Revenge
- Ⓓ Education

GO ON ➡

Informational

12. How would this article be best described?

- Ⓐ A biography
- Ⓑ A short story
- Ⓒ Historical fiction
- Ⓓ An autobiography

13. What is the author's purpose in presenting the information in the first paragraph? How does it relate to the overall passage? Use examples from the text to support your answer.

Write your answer in complete sentences.

_____
_____
_____
_____
_____
_____
_____

Informational

14. According to the passage, *Moby Dick* was Melville's masterpiece. How do you know the book was not a bestseller? Give examples from the text to support your answer.

Write your answer in complete sentences.

_____
_____
_____
_____
_____
_____
_____

STOP

Literary

SESSION 2
Transition to ELA

In Session 2, you will read two poems and one literary passage:
- "Flying Fish" by Carl Sandburg
- "Flying Fish" by Mary McNeil Fenollosa
- The Adventures of Mando's Watch

There are multiple-choice and short written response questions for you to answer after each passage. Read the passages as often as you need to. Then answer the questions. Keep working until you see the word STOP at the bottom of page 176.

SESSION 2 — Transition to ELA

Literary

Directions
Read the poems and answer questions 15 through 21.

Flying Fish
by Carl Sandburg

1 I have lived in many half-worlds myself…and so I know you.

2 I leaned at a deck rail watching a monotonous sea, the same circling birds and the same plunge of furrows carved by the plowing keel.

3 I leaned so…and you fluttered struggling between two waves in the air now…and then under the water and out again…a fish…a bird…a fin thing…a wing thing.

4 Child of water, child of air, fin thing and wing thing…I have lived in many half-worlds myself…and so I know you.

Flying Fish
by Mary McNeil Fenollosa

1 Out where the sky and the sky-blue sea
    Merge in a mist of sheen,
There started a vision of silver things,
A leap and a quiver, a flash of wings
    The sky and the sea between.

2 Is it of birds from the blue above,
    Or fish from the depths that be?
      Or is it the ghosts
      In silver hosts
Of birds that were drowned at sea?

GO ON ➡

Literary

15. In the first poem, by Sandburg, where is the speaker?

- Ⓐ On the shore
- Ⓑ In a boat
- Ⓒ At home
- Ⓓ Swimming

16. In the first stanza of the poem by Fenollosa, what does the speaker notice?

- Ⓐ Something moving above the water
- Ⓑ Fish swimming just below the surface
- Ⓒ Birds flying overhead
- Ⓓ Ghosts

17. In contrast to Fenollosa's poem, what is true of the speaker in Sandburg's poem?

- Ⓐ He is just an observer.
- Ⓑ He thinks he can fly.
- Ⓒ He identifies with the fish.
- Ⓓ He wants to catch the fish.

GO ON

SESSION 2 Transition to ELA

Literary

18. Read this line from Sandburg's poem:

    "...and the same plunge of furrows carved by the plowing keel."

    What does the rhythm of this line imitate?

    Ⓐ The flying fish
    Ⓑ The birds circling above
    Ⓒ The rocking of the boat
    Ⓓ The smooth surface of the sea

19. What is the rhyme scheme for each stanza of Fenollosa's poem?

    Ⓐ ABCDE
    Ⓑ ABBCC
    Ⓒ ABCCA
    Ⓓ ABCCB

GO ON

Literary

SESSION 2 Transition to ELA

20. What does Sandburg mean when he says "I have lived in many half-worlds myself…"? Give examples from the poem to support your answer.

Write your answer in complete sentences.

SESSION 2 Transition to ELA

Literary

21. In the second stanza of the Fenollosa poem, the author questions what it was she saw. Why is the author uncertain about what she has seen? Give examples from the poem to support your answer.

Write your answer in complete sentences.

_____
_____
_____
_____
_____
_____
_____

Literary

Directions
Read the passage and answer questions 22 through 28.

The Adventures of Mando's Watch
by Carlos Perez

1   My father's name is Armando Rafael Arturo Perez. It's important that you know that, because his name plays a crucial role in this story. Last week, his parents—my grandparents—got a phone call all the way from Scotland. This is how my grandmother described the conversation. Imagine a ringing telephone.

2   "Hello?" said my grandmother Rosa.

3   "I'm sorry to bother you," said a woman with a strong accent. "My name is Megan Douglas, and I'm calling from Glasgow, Scotland. Is there a little boy there named Armando Rafael Arturo Perez?"

4   "Little boy? That's our son's name, but he's not little—he's 45 years old. Why are you calling?"

5   A long pause followed this question, and then the caller replied. "I'm afraid I'm a wee bit confused," she said. "You see, I have a Mickey Mouse watch here with that name engraved on the back. Underneath the name it says, 'Frewsburg, New York.' I thought a small boy might have lost it."

6   Now the long pause was on the *other* end of the line. I can picture the expression on my grandmother's face, like a person in a movie who steps out of a time machine and runs into herself at a younger age. "Where did you say you found this watch?"

7   "I didn't yet say, actually," said the caller. "The truth is, my son Davey bought it from an auction site on the Internet. It was sold by a man who found it in a thrift shop in Lancaster, England. But when it arrived and we saw the engraving, we thought a child might be missing it, so we did some searching and found your number."

GO ON

Literary

8 "You're right that a child missed that watch," my grandmother said. "Mando—that's our son—was so upset about it. But that was 35 years ago! How did it end up in England after all these years?"

9 "Where did he lose it?" asked the woman.

10 "We had taken a trip to Disney World," said my grandmother. "When we got there, we told Mando and his brothers they could each pick one special souvenir, and Mando picked that watch. They engraved it in the shop where we bought it. He was so excited." My grandmother was quiet for a moment, remembering.

11 "Then what happened?"

12 "Then we went to eat. Mando put the package down next to his chair. Just as we were finishing, a parade went by. We all ran to see it and forgot about the watch. We didn't remember it for at least an hour, and then it was too late. We searched everywhere, but it was gone."

13 "Until now," said the woman. "I'll send it to you, and you can give it back to its rightful owner!"

14 A week after the call, my grandparents invited our family to dinner. As we were eating dessert, my grandmother brought out a little box and handed it to my father.

15 "Go ahead, open it," she said.

16 My father was puzzled. It wasn't his birthday or Father's Day. He opened the box. And then about ten different emotions chased each other across his face. He was speechless, and he looked like he might actually cry. That's when my grandmother told us the story.

17 "I still don't understand how it got to England," I said.

18 "Only the watch knows the answer to that question," said my grandmother. "And I'm afraid the only thing it's going to tell us is the time!"

GO ON

Literary

SESSION 2
Transition to ELA

22. Whose voice introduces the story?
- Ⓐ Mando's son
- Ⓑ Mando's father
- Ⓒ Mando's grandfather
- Ⓓ Mando's grandmother

23. Which character recovered the watch?
- Ⓐ Rosa
- Ⓑ Carlos
- Ⓒ Davey
- Ⓓ Mando

24. What did Megan Douglas have of Mando's that allowed her to trace the watch to its owner?
- Ⓐ His wallet
- Ⓑ His school records
- Ⓒ His original bill of sale
- Ⓓ His full name and address

GO ON ➡

SESSION 2 Transition to ELA

Literary

25. What did Mando feel when his mother handed him the box with the watch in it?

    Ⓐ Fear and anxiety
    Ⓑ Relief and security
    Ⓒ Anger and frustration
    Ⓓ Surprise and pleasure

26. Where had the watch probably been during the years since Mando saw it last?

    Ⓐ All over the world
    Ⓑ In a child's toy box
    Ⓒ At an auction house
    Ⓓ In a safe deposit box

GO ON ➡

Literary

27. Describe the sequence of events the watch went through from the time Mando received it until it was returned to him. Use details from the passage to support your answer.

Write your answer in complete sentences.

_____
_____
_____
_____
_____
_____
_____

SESSION 2 — Transition to ELA

Literary

28. How does the author show that the Perez family is close and loving? Use details from the passage to support your answer.

Write your answer in complete sentences.

_____
_____
_____
_____
_____
_____
_____

STOP